Ditch the Donkey

Unusual holidays in the usual destinations

Ditch the Donkey

Unusual holidays in the usual destinations

Paul Jenner & Christine Smith

Editors Richard Craze, Roni Jay

new tricks for old dogs

Published by White Ladder Press Ltd
Great Ambrook, Near Ipplepen, Devon TQ12 5UL
01803 813343
www.whiteladderpress.com

First published in Great Britain in 2006

10 9 8 7 6 5 4 3 2 1

© Paul Jenner and Christine Smith 2006

The right of Paul Jenner and Christine Smith to be identified as authors of this work has
been asserted by them in accordance with the Copyright, Designs and Patents Act 1988.

ISBN 1 905410 02 6
ISBN 978 1 905410 02 6

British Library Cataloguing in Publication Data
A CIP record for this book can be obtained from the British Library.

All rights reserved. No part of this publication may be reproduced, stored in a retrieval system, or transmitted in any form or by any means, electronic, mechanical, photocopying,
recording, or otherwise without either the prior written permission of the Publishers or a
licence permitting restricted copying in the United Kingdom issued by the Copyright
Licensing Agency Ltd, 90 Tottenham Court Road, London W1P 0LP. This book may not be
lent, resold, hired out or otherwise disposed of by way of trade in any form of binding or
cover other than that in which it is published, without the prior consent of the Publishers.

Designed and typeset by Julie Martin Ltd
Cover design by Julie Martin Ltd
Cover illustration by Sue Misselbrook
Printed and bound by TJ International Ltd, Padstow, Cornwall

White Ladder Press
Great Ambrook, Near Ipplepen, Devon TQ12 5UL
01803 813343
www.whiteladderpress.com

Contents

KEY

A = Adults	✓ = Yes	Sp = Spring	1 = Budget
C = Children alone	✗ = No	S = Summer	2 = Medium
F = Families	All = Various	A = Autumn	3 = Expensive
		W = Winter	All = Various

	Holiday	Best For	Active	When	Cost
1	Underknown islands	A/F	All	Sp S A W	All
2	Messing about in boats	A/F	✓	S A	All
3	On the cut	A/F	✓	Sp S A	1 2
4	Out of season	A	All	W	1 2
5	Up a mountain	A/F	All	S A	All
6	In the desert	A	All	Sp A W	All
7	Bogs, marshes and swamps	A/F	All	Sp S A W	All
8	Staying in a monastery	A	✗	Sp S A W	1
9	Hidden and secret places	A	✗	Sp S A W	All
10	Horsing around	A/F	✓	Sp S A W	All
11	Putting a horse before a cart	A/F	✓	S	1
12	Travels with a donkey and others	A/F	✓	S	2
13	Pat a manatee and other nature holidays	A/F	✓	Sp S A W	2 3
14	A bird in your hand	A	✓	Sp S A W	2
15	Working holidays with animals	A	✓	Sp S A W	1 2
16	Farm holidays	A/F	All	S	1
17	Hiking	A	✓	Sp S A	1
18	Cycling and mountain biking	A	✓	Sp S A	All
19	Swimming	A	✓	S	2
20	Snorkelling	A/F	✓	S A	All
21	Surfing	A	✓	Sp S A W	All
22	Windsurfing and dinghy sailing	A/F	✓	S	All
23	Canoeing and sea kayaking	A/F	✓	S	1 2
24	Sports clinics	A/F	✓	Sp S A W	All
25	Learn the language	A	✗	Sp S A W	1
26	Arts and crafts	A	✗	Sp S A	1 2
27	Music, theatre and dance	A/C	All	Sp S A W	All
28	Time travel	A	All	Sp S A	2 3
29	Food, wine and grape picking	A	All	Sp S A W	All
30	Educating Rita... and Richard	A/C	✗	S	3
31	Make the world a better place	A	✓	S	All

	Holiday	Best For	Active	When	Cost
32	Alternative holidays	A	All	Sp S A	2
33	Spas	A	All	Sp S A W	2 3
34	The pilgrimage to Santiago de Compostela	A	✓	Sp S A	2
35	Freediving	A	✓	S A	2
36	Scuba diving	A	✓	S A	1 2
37	Canyoning	A/F	✓	S	1 2
38	Caving	A/F	✓	Sp S A W	1 2
39	Skydiving	A	✓	S	2 3
40	Gliding	A	✓	S	2 3
41	Climbing and mountaineering	A/F	✓	Sp S A W	1 2
42	Music and arts festivals	A	✗	S	2 3
43	Carnivals and fiestas	A/F	✗	Sp S A W	All
44	Famous footsteps	A/F	✗	Sp S A	All
45	Cruising	A/F	✗	Sp S A W	3
46	Family activity holidays	F	✓	S	1 2
47	Theme parks you've never heard of	A/F	✗	Sp S A	All
48	Children's clubs	C	✓	Sp S A	All
49	Home alone	C	✓	Sp S A	1 2
50	Dirty weekends	A	✓	Sp S A W	2 3
51	Seeing fireworks	A/F	✗	Sp S A W	All
52	Venice the second time around	A	All	Sp S A	3
53	Getting married... and divorced	A	✗	Sp S A W	3
54	Romantic train journeys	A	✗	Sp S A W	3
55	Romantic Highway 1	A	All	Sp S A W	2 3
56	Romantic hotels	A	✗	Sp S A W	2 3
57	Pen pals	A	✗	Sp S A W	1
58	House swapping	A/F	✗	Sp S A W	1
59	Clubbing with a difference	A	All	Sp S A W	1
60	Downhill skiing	A/F	✓	W	2 3
61	Snowboarding	A/F	✓	W	2 3
62	Cross country skiing and snowshoeing	A	✓	W	All
63	Ski touring	A	✓	W	1 2
64	Dog mushing	A/F	✓	W	3

Introduction

This book is for you if you're looking for something unusual and different to do for your holiday, *but without having to go somewhere 'exotic'*. The destinations we've covered are those most popular with British tourists – Spain, France, Ireland, the USA (mostly Florida, New York and California), Greece, Germany, Italy, the Netherlands, Belgium, Portugal and Turkey. Occasionally we let other countries slip in if they've got something really special to offer and are easy to get to.

We've had great fun compiling this book. Some of our favourite unusual holidays include rounding up a herd of bison in France, staying in a monastery, painting in Monet's garden, swimming round the Greek islands, a New York Film Academy summer camp and the Tomatina festival in Spain, where people pelt one another with tomatoes.

Nobody has paid to be mentioned in this book. It's our own personal selection based on years of travelling.

Only a few of these holidays are available through the major tour operators. We give you contact details for the small, specialist tour operators and the local hotels (website and telephone number *except* where enquiries/bookings can be made only online). Quite often you'll have to make your own travel arrangements. You can easily do this via a travel agent or on the internet. As far as the larger hotels are concerned, note that you'll seldom get the best price by booking direct. You'll also find all this information online, where we can update it easily, at **www.whiteladderpress.com** (click on the Useful Contacts page alongside the information about this book). Here are some useful internet sites:

www.abta.com Insert the name of your chosen destination to be provided with a list of Association of British Travel Agents members that go to it.

www.holidaywizard.co.uk Order brochures.

www.expedia.co.uk Be your own travel agent and make your own air, hotel and car rental bookings.

www.lastminute.com; **www.icelolly.com**; **www.holidaywarehouse.co.uk** Deals on late bookings and cancellations.

www.tripadvisor.com, **www.thisistravel.com**; **www.reviewcentre.com** News and reviews by other holidaymakers.

www.weather.com The weather anywhere in the world.

www.saynoto0870.com Lists the ordinary numbers for many companies that have 0870 numbers (on which they may make around 1.5p a minute or even more when you call them).

A word on prices. We give approximate figures in pounds sterling *as a rough guide only*. Due to fluctuating exchange rates and other factors the actual price you pay at the time of booking may be slightly different.

We've tried every one of the ideas in the book but, obviously, it isn't possible to have experienced every single operator and stayed at every hotel. We provide contact details only as a starting point and we'd certainly encourage you to shop around and do as much research as possible. Who you book with is entirely your decision. We cannot take any responsibility for the quality of service you receive.

So go on! Ditch the donkey! Take a different kind of holiday this year.

Chapter 1

Castaway Holidays

Unusual holidays in this chapter: little known islands, flotillas, skippered charters, bareboats, rivers, canals and much more.

Who hasn't sometimes dreamed of a beautiful and *deserted* beach or of a lonely riverbank? In fact, you don't have to go to the South Seas to find what you want.

Unusual Holiday No. 1: Underknown Islands

You're sitting outside The Old Forge while the setting sun turns the waters of Loch Nevis an even deeper colour than the pint of Red Cuillin on the table. Rhona brings you a prawn and seafood platter and just at that moment a couple of Highland cattle stroll past your table. Welcome to the remotest pub on the British mainland (**www.theoldforge.co.uk** Tel: 01687 462 267). And that's official – according to the Guinness Book of Records. *Mainland*, did we hear you query? Well, yes, but it's an island according to everything but the dictionary. This pub stands on a peninsula whose fourth side is guarded by some of the most difficult wilderness in Britain. You won't find it on a road map because there's no road. You could hike it, if you're fit enough, but with luggage the only way is by boat from Mallaig (45 mins).

This is Inverie, Knoydart, one of the most isolated corners of Scotland or, come to that, the Earth. And yet you're still in a country with one of the world's highest population densities (about 250 people per square kilometre, since you ask). Of course, there are a few other people around – a handful of crazy locals and some hill walkers, but Knoydart proves that in Britain today you can still get as far from the madding crowd as when Gray wrote his famous elegy in 1751. Unless you're seeking hermit like solitude, this is about as good as it gets anywhere in the world.

And unlike a lot of wilderness you don't have to view it round a tent flap. At Knoydart sybarites are in luck. Fifteen minutes from The Old Forge, on foot, is the Kilchoan estate, with a choice of rather civilised self catering accommodation (**www.kilchoanknoydart. com** Tel: 01687 462 724). There's the Farmhouse, the Fank and the Barn (and we won't talk about the Druim Bothy which provides utterly authentic hardship). Another possibility is Stone Lodge at Doune out on the western end of the Knoydart peninsula (**www.doune-knoydart.co.uk** Tel: 01687 462 667). It's a bit further to hike to the pub but you can always hire a boat, which is the best way of getting around in these parts.

From Doune your eye may be caught by spectacular mountains dropping more than a thousand metres into the foam. Those are the Cuillin Hills and that is a *real* island, Skye, the most spectacular in the Hebrides. This is seriously moving scenery, the equal of Norway's fjords and far too tempting to be ignored. So it's back to the ferryman and onwards. Hotels on the island include the elegant Kinloch Lodge (**www.kinloch-lodge.co.uk** Tel: 01471 833 214) and the atmospheric Eilean Iarmain (**www.eileaniarmain.co.uk** Tel: 01471 833 332). But the ubiquitous boatmen of Mallaig and other ports are no longer the only means of reaching that mystical island. Nowadays there's also the impressive Skye Bridge, for which Kintail Lodge at Glenshiel makes a memorable base (**www. kintaillodgehotel.co.uk** Tel: 01599 511 275).

The problem with bridges is that they're too easy. Skye would no longer be a safe refuge for Bonnie Prince Charlie and maybe not for you. So it's on yet again, seasickness tablets ever ready, to Rhum, Lewis, and North and South Uist with one of the most beautiful and unspoilt beaches in the world (try the Orasay Inn **www.witb.co.uk/orasayinn.htm** Tel: 0187 061 0298 or Lochboisdale Hotel **www.lochboisdale.com** Tel: 0187 870 0332).

*

Britain's answer to Greek Island Hopping (see below) is the Isles of Scilly, an archipelago of more than 200 islands and islets flung into the teeth of an Atlantic gale 28 miles off Land's End. You'll arrive by helicopter from Penzance or by small aircraft. If you come by ferry you won't bring your car – they're not welcome here. You'll get around by boat, on foot, by bus or by taxi. St Mary's – the largest island at two and a half miles by one and three-quarters – may already be far away from it all but as it's home to three-quarters of the combined population of just 2,000, we'll move on to Tresco, the second largest and with a surprising range of scenery. The Tresco Island Hotel is the place to go (**www.tresco.co.uk/holidays/island_ hotel.asp** Tel: 01720 422 883), a colonial style building on the water's edge, looking out over uninhabited islands and the Golden Ball reef. Still not far enough? Then it has to be Bryher, the last of the five inhabited islands, where Hell Bay is the most inappropriately named location on the planet. This is a serious contender for the title of paradise. A beautiful hotel, beautifully furnished (Barbara Hepworth, Ivon Hitchens, Julian Trevelyan…) on a beautiful, rock rimmed bay looking out to where the Atlantic surf breaks like snow (**www.tresco.co.uk/holidays/hell_bay** Tel: 01720 422 947).

*

There was a whitewashed 'cubist' village with an exquisite ruined acropolis above. Meanwhile, on the beach below, there was not a soul and only one yacht swinging gently on its chain. It was said to belong to Paul Anka who, at that time in the mid-60s, was a famous singer and songwriter. The place was called Líndhos. Now, everything that was beautiful about it has been destroyed in the creation of one of the most popular resorts on the island of Rhodes. Those whitewashed village houses have all become holiday villas and hotels, the beach is crowded and there's scarcely room in the bay to fit another boat in.

Líndhos has gone forever but there are still a few Greek islands like Líndhos was 40 years ago. Where? Spread out a map and look for small islands at a significant distance from anything popular (because, otherwise, day trippers will be there too). Check the contours. You don't want anything too flat otherwise they'll have built an airport before you get there. And a water shortage would be helpful, to discourage development. In the Cyclades, Síkinos, Kímolos and Anáfi more or less fit the bill. In the Dodecanese, Kássos, Kárpathos, Hálki, Kastellórizo, Sími, Tílos and Léros come close, as do Ikaría (where Icarus fell into the sea) and Foúrni in the east and north Aegean.

There are plenty of websites offering advice. Try putting 'Greek island hopping' into your browser. A fun idea is **www.greecetravel. com/island-hopping-club**. They'll provide you with a mobile phone so that, when you're tired of one island, you can phone them to book your ferry and accommodation for the next one. A company called Island Wandering specialises in organising tailor-made itineraries (**www.islandwandering.com** Tel: 0870 777 9944). At the simplest you can set off with a selection of vouchers and use them when and where you please on more than 50 islands, or you can have everything precisely prebooked.

*

Italy has quite a lot of unknown islands. Unknown to the British, that is. The Italians know about them, of course, but they're keeping quiet. Who could place Panarea or Ústica on the map, or even knew they weren't diseases? We thought so.

Everybody knows Sicily, thanks to the public relations efforts of the Mafia, but all around, due to volcanic activity, are delightful small islands still not discovered by international package tourism.

Just to the north of Sicily lie the Aeolian Islands also known as the Lipari Islands. Lipari itself *has* been discovered but Panarea, easily the most ravishing, remains a little gem. To be frank, the beautiful people, who aren't slow to spot a good thing, have turned it into a bit of a St Tropez in August but outside the high season you'll have the scenery mostly to yourself. For accommodation try the Hotel Piazza (**www.hotelpiazza.it** Tel: 00 39 090 983 154).

Off the western tip of Sicily lie the Égadi or Aegadian Islands (to which Headwater runs a walking tour). Favignani is the largest (Albergo Ristorante Egadi Tel: 00 39 0923 921 232) but certainly not the quietest. For that try wild Marettimo or craggy Levanzo which, at just six square kilometres, is the smallest of the lot, bisected by a single road north to south (Albergo Pensione dei Fenici Tel: 00 39 0923 924 083).

Ústica lies north of the Égadi in quite splendid isolation, its indented coastline perfect for snorkelling and diving. Its 810 hectares are home to just 1,370 people, which leaves plenty of room for you.

Pantelleria, to the south-west of Sicily and just 30 miles off the coast of Tunisia, is relatively unspoilt because it has no sandy beaches. But in compensation it has some of the most unbelievably transparent waters in the Med. It's like swimming in glass. There are modern hotels but the best place to stay is a *dammuso*, a traditional style house built from the island's black volcanic rock and with a domed roof designed to capture rainwater (**www.dammusial mare.it/english/index.htm**).

Linosa and Lampedusa are the main Pelagie Islands, even further to the south, separated by some 50 km of glittering emerald sea. Lampedusa has seen a lot of development but Linosa, which has a population of 400, hardly any (**www.emmeti.it/Welcome/Sicilia/ Pelagie/Linosa/index.uk.html** and **www.linosa.too.it**). If you're there in August/September you may get to see turtles laying their eggs and the little clones scrambling down the Pozzolana di Ponente beach to take their chance of growing up. It's best to stay in one of the brightly painted village houses (Cavallaro travel agency, Tel: 00 39 0922 972 062); if you're a diver **www.marenos trumdiving.it** (Tel: 00 39 328 169 8697) can make all the arrangements for you.

Capraia in the Tuscan Islands is something truly special. To the north of the far more famous Elba, it's not to be confused with Capraia in the Trémiti Islands. *This* Capraia, unlike the other, has escaped development due to its rugged geography (the name comes from the Roman *capra* or goat). Amounting to some 20 square kilometres, only the village of Capraia is inhabited and although the port in summer is full of yachtsmen and divers you can have the rest of the island to yourself. There's a four star hotel, Il Saracino (Tel: 00 39 0586 905 018), and the three star Da Beppone (Tel: 00 39 0586 905 001).

Giglio, the second largest of the Tuscan Islands after Elba, has to be ruled out in August when it's packed with tourists and day trippers from Rome. But it's a genuine getaway most of the year, especially if you avoid Giglio Porto and Giglio Campese, where the hotels are, and instead take a room in the interior in Giglio Castello where thick walls protected the maze of medieval passages from pirate attack.

A good way of seeing all of the Tuscan Islands is by boat. The beautiful 67 foot schooner Isla Negra II visits Elba, Capraia, Giglio and Giannutri during a week long voyage (**www.islanegra.it** Tel: 00 39 330 268 400).You can also charter a yacht, bareboat or skippered, from **www.sail-italy.com** Tel: 01728 747 340.

Caprera, one of the Maddalena Islands, lies close enough to the north-east corner of Sardinia to be joined to it by a bridge. That's the bad news. The good news is that Garibaldi, the 19th Century hero of Italian unification, used to own the island and kept it to himself. Now a wildlife sanctuary, it has plenty of visitors but the only place to stay, and the only development apart from Garibaldi's house, is a Club Med.

Further information

For more about Scottish islands see **www.undiscoveredscotland.co.uk**, **www.scotland-inverness.co.uk** and **www.hotelreviewscotland.com**. For Greek islands see **www.greek-islands.eu.com**, **www.greekislandhopping.com**, **www.greekbackpack.com** and **www.cycladestravel.com**.

Some specialist operators

Scotland

www.noble-caledonia.co.uk Tel: 020 7752 0000

www.celtictrails.co.uk Tel: 0131 448 2869
www.wildernessscotland.com Tel: 0131 625 6635
www.rabbies.com Tel: 0131 226 3133
www.bruceshighlandtours.co.uk Tel: 01397 702 016

Isles of Scilly
www.islesofscillyholidays.co.uk Tel: 01720 423 239
www.ios-travel.co.uk Tel: 0845 710 5555

Greece
www.greeksun.co.uk Tel: 01732 740 317
www.hidden-greece.co.uk Tel: 020 7839 2553
www.kosmar.com Tel: 0870 700 0747
www.laskarina.co.uk Tel: 01444 880 380
www.sunisle.co.uk Tel: 0871 222 1226

Italy
Panarea www.mediterraneo.it Tel: 00 39 091 690 0824
Marettimo www.crusadertravel.com Tel: 020 8744 0474
Égadi Islands www.headwater.com Tel: 01606 720 099
Ústica www.thesicilianexperience.co.uk Tel: 020 782 89171
Aeolian Islands www.thesicilianexperience.co.uk Tel: 020 782 89171
Pantelleria www.calltour.it Tel: 00 39 0923 911065
Caprera www.clubmed.co.uk Tel: 0700 258 2932

Some questions to ask

✔ How do we get to the island – by plane, ferry or bridge?
✔ How long does it take from the mainland?
✔ Is it easy to get to other islands in the archipelago?
✔ What's the population of the island?
✔ When is peak season?
✔ Are there high-rise developments?
✔ Are there lots of sandy beaches or is everything concentrated on just one?
✔ Is traffic allowed on the island?
✔ How do we get around?
✔ What is there to do on the island?
✔ Are there shops for all needs?

✓ Does it rain much – and what do we do when it does?

✓ Are there nightclubs/discotheques?

Who are underknown island holidays for?

Romantics, beachcombers, poets, seekers after tranquillity… For the Scottish islands it helps if you like rain.

Pros

• The more inaccessible the island the more unspoilt.

Cons

• A small, remote island can seem more like a trap than an escape.

Where to go

In addition to the above, there are more islands than you'd ever imagine.

England: Lundy Island, three miles long and half a mile wide in the Bristol Channel, has a range of accommodation where Long John Silver would have felt quite at home (**www.lundyisland. co.uk** Tel: 01271 863 636). Lindisfarne, off the Northumberland Coast, is a marvellous place to see Brent geese, whooper swans and widgeon in winter (**www.thenorth-east.fsnet.co.uk/ Lindisfarne.htm** – try the Lindisfarne Hotel **www.lindisfarne. org.uk** Tel: 01289 389 273).

Wales: Bardsey Island is more popular with migrating birds than people (**www.totaltravel.co.uk** Tel: 0845 811 2233).

Ireland: Achill Island is spoilt by a bridge to the mainland but the Aran Islands (**www.visitaranislands.com** and **www.aranislandshotel.com**) and Clare Island (**www.anu.ie/clareisland/welcome.htm**) aren't; for a specialist tour operator try **www.authenticireland.com** Tel: 00 353 65 684 4941 or see **www.indexireland. com**.

France: Of the Iles du Ponant off the Brittany coast (**www.iles-du-ponant.com**), Houat (Hotel La Sirène Tel: 00 33 2 97 30 66 73) is much smaller and less well known than nearby Belle-Ile, while little Molène (Hotel Kastell an Daol Tel: 00 33 2 98 07 39 11) is a better bet than larger Ouessant; Ile de Bréhat is probably the best place of all to escape, its 318 hectares free from all traffic except tractors (**www.hotel-bellevue-brehat .com** Tel: 00 33 2 96 200 005). Who would have thought that just a little way from Cannes there would be a beautiful island with a wonderful beach and no tourism development at all? But there is a snag. Where to stay on St Honorat? We'll tell you how in Chapter 2 (see Staying In A Monastery). Of the nearby Iles d'Or, Port-Cros is the smallest, the most mountainous and the wildest because its 750 hectares are all *Parc National*; Le Manoir d'Hélène is the only hotel (**http://monsite.wanadoo.fr/ hotelmanoirportcros/page8.html** Tel: 00 33 4 9405 9052).

Netherlands: Vliehand and Schiermonnikoog are the quietest Frisian Islands (**www.reiswijs.co.uk**).

Spain: Formentera is the least visited of the Balearic Islands with long white sandy beaches, tiny coves and impressive cliffs (**www.formentera.co.uk** Tel: 01642 210 163).

Portugal: The Azores are already pretty remote being 1,000 odd miles out in the Atlantic, but the islands of Pico and Corvo as well as parts of the larger São Jorge should satisfy most hermits (general information **www.azores.com**; for a specialist operator try **www.azoreschoice.com** Tel: 01768 775 672).

Florida: The 106 mile long Keys attract some four million tourists a year (**www.thefloridakeys.com**) but Pine Island, an 'inner island' with more mangroves than sand, is a quieter alternative (**www.pineislandfl.com**).

California: The Channel Islands off the coast between Santa Barbara and Los Angeles are National Park with absolutely no development. But you can stay as long as you're willing to camp (**www.nps.gov/chis**). If you want to be on a protected island but in a little more luxury then Catalina Island is for you (see Chapter 10: Romantic Holidays).

When

Early summer or early autumn in the Mediterranean, to be truly alone. August is a quiet and cheap month on Florida's islands but between June and November there's always a risk of hurricanes.

Price guide

Expect to pay from around £500 per person per week for a fully inclusive island holiday, up to £2,000 in a luxury hotel in the USA. Holidays to Marettimo cost from around £300 for seven nights, self catering without flights. Individual hotels, per person per night half board: Stone Lodge at Doune around £50; The Tresco Island Hotel £125-£250; The Hotel Piazza on Panarea around £145; The Manoir d'Hélène, Port Cros, around £150. A berth on a schooner visiting the Tuscan Islands will cost from £500 to around £1,100 a week; on a cruise ship to the Hebrides £3,000.

Unusual Holiday No. 2: Messing About In Boats

There is nothing – absolutely nothing – half so much worth doing as simply messing about in boats, as Ratty told Mole in *The Wind in the Willows*. How right he was. And he might have added that nothing – absolutely nothing – is half so good for getting away from it all. Of course, unless you're capable of skippering your own boat you'll still have to see the crew and other passengers but with the right kind of craft that needn't be too onerous.

Our preference is sailing, but, of course, you can equally mess about in motor boats which tend to be more spacious, not to say faster. Never imagine, though, that the words 'private cabin' imply the sort of thing you'd get on a cruise liner. Envisage something more like a cupboard. Whatever style you choose you'll have no problem finding some water to yourself out at sea. On the coast it's a different matter. The islands mentioned above are your quietest option but the best advice is to avoid the six weeks from the middle of July to the end of August.

There are basically four ways of going about it: flotilla, sailing school, skippered and bareboat.

A *flotilla* is the way to get your hands on the tiller if you haven't got a qualification or much experience (although some flotilla companies do insist on a minimum of knowledge). All explanations will be given at the initial briefing and there'll be people on the lead boat to sort you out if you get into problems. Some boats will be arranged for two people (say a Jaguar 27, for example). But others will be for four up to maybe eight which means that, if you're a couple, you'll be sharing. And, of course, you'll be expected to stick, more or less, with the group, anchoring together at midday and again in the evening. Whether or not that constitutes being a castaway is up to you. If you already know a bit about sailing, or learn quickly, some companies will let you off on your own once you've proved yourself.

A *sailing school* will be much more structured, with the emphasis on learning and getting a certificate. You may be sleeping on the boat or you could have accommodation ashore and make day cruises. Towards the end of your holiday you might be allowed to hire a school boat to sail on your own.

Skippered charter means you pay for a qualified person to take charge of the boat. Be clear about whether you want to join in handling the boat or just laze around. If the boat is large enough and you're rich enough you can have people take care of everything, including fixing your sundowner.

Bareboat is the ultimate freedom. It means you charter a yacht just for you and go where you please (within agreed limits). Obviously, no one is going to let you loose with an expensive yacht unless you have the necessary experience. A lot of companies insist on a paper qualification but, for those anarchic old sea dogs who have never bothered with that kind of thing, some will make their own judgement based on a written summary of your exploits and an assessment on the boat (it's pretty obvious who knows which way up a sail goes and who doesn't).

If you didn't know what bareboat meant but hoped it had something to do with going naked you can get in touch with like-minded American yachties at **www.bareboating.com**.

Finally, if you'd love a sailing holiday but can't afford one there is a cheaper way. For an annual fee, Crewseekers (**www.crewseekers. co.uk** Tel:01489 578 319) will find you crewing work. Also try Professional Yacht Deliveries Worldwide (**www.pydww.com** Tel:

01539 552130) or Reliance Yacht Management (**www.reliance-yachts.com** Tel:01252 378239).

Further information

Try **www.charternet.com** and **www.uk250.co.uk** for links to sailing holidays and charter companies. For the USA try **www.allthevacations.com** and then enter 'Florida yacht charters' or whatever else you want.

Some specialist operators

Flotilla
www.minotaurholidays.com Tel: 01785 285 434
www.realadventures.com Tel: 00 1 617 738 4700
www.fyly.gr Tel: 00 30 210 985 8670
www.sunsail.com Tel: 0870 777 0313

Bareboat
www.nauticsail.gr Tel: 00 30 210 982 30 29
www.sunsail.com Tel: 0870 777 0313
www.floridayacht.com Tel: 00 1 305 293 0800 (also a sailing school)

Skippered
www.nauticsail.gr Tel: 00 30 210 982 30 29
www.waterfantaseas.com Tel: 00 1 305 531 1480 (Miami) or 00 1 954 524 1234 (Fort Lauderdale)
www.swfyachts.com Tel: 00 1 239 656 1339

Sailing schools
www.boss-sail.co.uk Tel: 023 8045 7733
www.butesail.clara.net Tel: 01700 504 881
www.celticventures.com Tel: 00 353 402 39418
www.brittanysail.co.uk Tel: 00 33 2 9817 0131
www.canarysail.com Tel: 01438 880 890
www.euro-sail.co.uk Tel: 01473 833 001
www.blunosa.it Tel: 00 39 080 553 8808
www.sunsail.com Tel: 0870 770 6312
www.seafarercruises.com Tel: 0870 442 2447

www.centurionyachting.co.uk Tel: 0797 491 5944

Some questions to ask

✔ What sailing experience do I need?

✔ Do I need a paper qualification?

✔ Are you approved by the Royal Yachting Association?

✔ Do I have to stay with the flotilla all the time?

✔ If we're sharing boats, can we decide who we share with?

✔ How many hours sailing each day?

✔ What do I need to bring?

✔ Do we have to buy our own food?

✔ What happens if, for example, a sail is damaged by the wind?

✔ What happens if someone is sick or injured?

✔ Will I be insured?

Who are boating holidays for?

All kinds of people, actually, because there are so many different ways of going about it. The most important thing is a liking for the sea and a degree of immunity from seasickness.

Pros

● There's still plenty of wide open space out at sea.

Cons

● Seasickness – though this usually wears off after three days at most.
● There isn't much room on a boat to get away from fellow sailors.

Where to go

If you're thinking in terms of a flotilla you're limited to where they operate. The Ionian is ideal, with plenty of anchorages just a short distance apart. The Cyclades, too. For bareboat or skippered charter you have a lot more flexibility – in UK waters Cornwall, the Isles of Scilly and the Western Isles are the best; the south-west coast of Ireland; in the Med the Balearics, Corsica, Sardinia, the Tuscan Islands, Sicily and its islands. Southwest Florida, including the Florida Keys, is one of the top charter destinations in the world, a mass of islands and inlets with unrivalled facilities.

When

We've had some great sailing in the Med – and even in Britain – in the winter but the whole experience is generally much more enjoyable from May to October (but excepting overcrowded August). In the Florida Keys May can be good – June to November is hurricane season and November to April is high season.

Price guide

Flotilla holidays cost from around £400 up to about £1,500 per person for two weeks, including flights, depending on season and how many are sharing a boat. Bareboat charter is about the same and you'll also need to leave a security deposit of from a few hundred up to maybe £2,000, depending on the value of the boat. Fuel, port fees and food will be on top. A skipper will cost around £1,000 a week. At the top end, for a large yacht with skipper and crew to take care of everything the sky is the limit – or, should we say, the ocean.

Unusual Holiday No. 3: On The Cut

If you get involved in the world of narrowboats you'll soon learn to call the canal 'the cut' otherwise everyone will know you're just a prat on holiday.

For those who aren't familiar with it the canal system in Britain can come as a very pleasant surprise. For the most part hidden away from 'ordinary' people, some 2,000 miles of waterways criss-cross the country as if in a parallel world. There's a very relaxing speed limit of 4 mph. – to protect the banks from wash – but, in reality, you probably won't average more than 3 mph. which means that anyone who wants to stretch their legs can easily keep up. And when it's time to stop for the day you can tie up more or less anywhere on the towpath side (taking care not to obstruct a lock). There are no parking meters here.

Puttering along on water in the heart of the countryside with sheep and cows on either side is pleasantly bizarre. But quite a lot of enthusiasts adore the industrial landscapes just as much, especially if they're derelict. And just about everybody loves to find that special little pub by the lock gates.

Ah, yes, the locks. After the novelty has worn off, people end up either relishing them or hating them. For the former, the British canal system provides some formidable challenges – Delph, Bratch, Caen Hill, the Rothersthorpe Flight, the Wolverhampton 21. The rest begin to wonder why somebody didn't invent an easier way of coping with gradients. Well, somebody did. And you can see it, and use it, near Northwich in Cheshire. The Anderton Boat Lift is known as the 'Cathedral of the Canals' and was the world's first, using hydraulics to effectively lift a section of canal and its boats up and down. But that lift aside, you'll have to use a bit of elbow grease to open and close lock gates.

The traditional canal boat is, of course, the narrow boat, so called because British canals are, well, narrow and so the boats had to be as well. You can also hire small motor cruisers but, somehow, they're just not right. They go *wah-ah-aah* whilst a narrow boat makes a nice, contemplative *chug-chug-chug*. Real narrow boats are huge affairs stretching on, it seems, for miles. You'll probably hire something modern and shorter that sleeps four or, for a bigger family or group, eight.

Continental waterways, on the other hand, aren't narrow at all. Some of them, in fact, are quite frighteningly wide with significant currents. Well, the Continent is just so much *bigger*. So a narrow boat wouldn't be much good there. On the Continent motorboats that go *wah-ah-aah* are positively ideal.

Further information

You can find out almost everything you need to know from the links on **www.canals.com**. Also take a look at **www.britishwaterways.co.uk** and **www.waterscape.com**. For a one stop check on the availability of boats from some 30 companies go to **www.waterwaysholidays.com** (Tel: 0870 747 2934); **www.europeafloat.com** has an index of hire companies. If you like the idea of inland waterways but don't want canals take a look at **www.norfolkbroads.com**.

Some inland waterways companies:

www.viking-afloat.com Tel: 01905 610 660

www.napton-marina.co.uk Tel: 01926 813 644

www.kateboats.co.uk Tel: 01926 492 968

www.ashbyboats.co.uk Tel: 01455 212 671

www.waterways holidays.com Tel: 0870 747 2934 (UK, Ireland, France)

www.blakes.co.uk Tel: 0870 2202 498 (UK, France)

www.crownblueline.com Tel: 0870 160 5634 (UK, France, Germany, Netherlands, Italy)

www.swrecreation.com (California)

Some questions to ask

✓ Is the canal in a good state of repair? (Many aren't.)

✓ Is there enough water in the canal? (Some have sections which have become almost too shallow to navigate.)

✓ How many lock gates are there on this section of canal?

✓ How many pubs are there on this section of canal?

✓ Is there any form of heating?

✓ Do we have to empty the toilets?

✓ Where can I buy provisions?

✓ Are there any things to do along the canal/river?

✓ Are there marinas I can put into?

✓ What happens if there's a problem with the boat?

✓ Will I be insured in case of a collision?

Who are inland waterways holidays for?

Lovers of tradition, the British countryside and British pubs. Also the French countryside and a glass of *vin*. Also, well, any countryside really (and any tipple at all).

Pros

● Plenty of tranquillity.

● About as reasonable a holiday as you can get.

Cons

● Working the locks is pretty hard work.

● It can all get a bit grubby.

Where to go

In Britain the Llangollen Canal has everything to satisfy the unconvinced while the Caldon, especially the Consall Forge section, is by general consent one of the most beautiful canals in the country. Other good bets are the Southern Oxford, the Grand Union, the Staffs and Worcester, Titford, the Leeds and Liverpool, Rochdale, and, in Scotland, the Forth and Clyde canals. For motor boating on inland waterways abroad try the Shannon and Erne in Ireland; the Muritz Lake region of northern Germany; and in France, Alsace-Lorraine, the Garonne in Aquitaine, the 400 miles of waterways in Brittany, the Camargue (for white horses, black bulls and pink flamingos), the Lot (gorges), the Loire/Nivernais (chateaux) and the Canal du Midi. Florida is a paradise for inland waterways; in California go to Shasta Lake which is set in a wilderness of half a million acres.

When

Most European operators open for business in May and run through to October. Florida's summer hurricane season may be worth risking on dry land but less so on water. California's Shasta Lake is not for the winter.

Price guide

A narrow boat for four costs from around £500 up to £1,000 a week and for eight from around £750 up to £1,500, so reckon on £100-£200 a head if the boat is full (but you might not consider that as getting away from it all). Motor boats are similar but the truly luxurious can cost much more. Shasta Lake, California will cost from around £1,000 a week for a houseboat for 10 in spring/autumn up to as much as £4,000 a week for a houseboat sleeping 20 in summer. In all cases travel and food will be on top.

Unusual Holiday No. 4: Out Of Season

The simplest way of getting away from it all is to go out of season. It's not as crazy as it sounds. It doesn't have to mean going in the rain or the cold. The fact is we've all become conditioned to take our holidays at specific times – in August, basically – not necessarily for any logical reason at all. Remember that the longest day (and therefore the most intense sunshine) is in June.

Anywhere you go in the low season you'll find not just more elbow room but also lower prices. The effect is at its greatest in beach resorts. In other words, cities like London are busy all year. Their attractions aren't so dependent on the weather and it's not just holidaymakers bidding for rooms but business travellers and students, too. On the other hand, beach resorts, especially those that have no industry other than tourism, are utterly transformed by the arrival of September.

For several years now we've lived just behind the beaches of the Costa Brava but you'll be unlikely to see us on the coast in August. Come September it's a different story. In fact, it's like a completely different world. We can find beaches to ourselves once again. And it's not only that. The roads leading to the beaches are suddenly quiet. There's no problem getting a table at favourite restaurants. The food and service are better and even the wine (we know of restaurants and bars that water down the house wine in summer and put cheap liquor into the empty bottles of expensive brands). We carry on swimming, without any discomfort, until the middle of October. In the eastern Mediterranean, where water temperatures are a few degrees higher, you can swim even later. Waters around Cyprus tend to be a mildly bracing 17°C in early winter, only five degrees less than the Costa Brava in summer. In fact, seas tend to be at their warmest at the beginning of September and don't reach their coldest until the end of February. In the Canary islands you can swim all year (winter water temperatures are around 17 or 18°C).

For hikers, too, autumn and spring are preferable to summer. In July and August it's just too darned hot. Even in the mountains there's not necessarily much respite. During the morning the heat evaporates water into huge, boiling clouds and in the afternoon it all falls to Earth again, accompanied by dangerous lightning. In September or October, by contrast, as well as January and February, the weather can remain stable for a fortnight or more at a time. You have the mountain to yourself (or, if it's winter, the lower slopes), the refuges are empty, the air is clear and you have *energy*.

When it comes to accommodation don't be shy about negotiating. Most hotels and especially self catering accommodation can be induced to give an extra discount in the low season.

Further information

To check what the weather will be like take a look at **www.weather.com**.

Some questions to ask
✔ When is the low season?
✔ Will everything be open?
✔ What will the weather be like?
✔ Is the room/apartment/house heated?
✔ What's the best price you can offer me?

Who are out of season holidays for?
Anyone who doesn't have children of school age.

Pros
● Fewer people.
● Lower prices.

Cons
● Some things may be shut.
● The weather may be unreliable.

Where to go
Everywhere, but especially beach resorts. Best bets in the Med for early or late season swimming are the Costa del Sol (but get well away from the Straits of Gibraltar where the cold Atlantic pours in), Sicily and its islands, Malta, Linosa, Crete, Cyprus, the Cyclades and the Dodecanese. In the Canaries you can swim all year round. Florida is one place you can escape the crowds in August because it's hurricane season (but, with a bit of luck, you'll never see one).

When

Not school holidays. For swimming, mid-September/mid-October is preferable to May/June because the water temperature will be several degrees higher.

Price guide

Prices out of season can be drastically lower. No-frills airline seats could be less than a quarter of the high season prices, while accommodation may be half.

And finally

Hirta, part of the St Kilda group, is the remotest inhabited island in Britain. In January 1891 a St Kildan sent a letter to a woman in London. In those days and at that rugged time of year the usual method was to put the letter in a hollowed out piece of wood, nail on a lid and launch it during a north-westerly. A few weeks was the norm for the 'St Kilda Mail' but this particular letter was finally delivered four years later in August 1895, having drifted all the way to Norway. Now surely that's the definition of getting away from it all. You'll need permission to stay from the National Trust for Scotland and, sorry, it won't be comfortable (Tel: 01463 232 034).

Other Castaway Holidays: See Chapter 3: Holidays With Animals; Chapter 4: Sport And Adventure Holidays; Chapter 6: Mind, Body And Spirit Holidays; Chapter 7: Extreme Holidays.

Chapter 2

Hideaway Holidays

Unusual holidays in this chapter: mountains, deserts, bogs, monasteries, secret places and much more.

Where, in this crowded world, can you hide yourself away? Mongolia? Alaska? Patagonia? In fact, it isn't necessary to do anything as drastic nor as distant.

Unusual Holiday No. 5: Up A Mountain

The top of a mountain is a great place to get away from it all but a terrible place to build a hotel. One way of escaping the rigours of the climate at 2,050 metres is to dig a tunnel, which is exactly what the Swiss Army did in the Gotthard Massif. When the military didn't need it any more a sociologist called Jean Odermatt had the idea of opening it as a hotel. Well, obviously. It's name *La Claustra* isn't short for claustrophobia but means 'monastery', apparently. Four thousand square metres of tunnels and caverns may not be everybody's idea of fun but the owner says his guests never want to leave (**www.claustra.ch/de/welcome.cfm** Tel: 00 41 91 880 5055).

If, having staggered up a mountain, you'd also like a bedroom with a bit of a view, then Mount Pilatus is a better bet. From your window in the three star Bellevue Hotel, more or less on the summit at 2,132 metres, you'll be able to look down at night on the twinkling lights of Lucerne and up at the twinkling stars, seeming to be twice as large as normal. The sister hotel, the larger and rather impregnable looking Pilatus, is just a few metres lower (**www.pilatus.com** Tel: 00 41 41 329 12 12).

Spain is second only to Switzerland in terms of its mean altitude. But its highest mountain isn't in the Pyrenees nor the Sierra Nevada, but on the little old island of Tenerife. El Teide is an impressive 3,710 metres and rather more than half way up is the Parador de Canadas el Teide, a grand mountain lodge with just 37 rooms. It's the only building inside the Parque Nacional del Teide (**www.paradores-spain.es** Tel: 00 34 922 374 841).

The practical problems of building and operating proper hotels up mountains means they're never going to be cheap. The budget answer is the refuge. The drawback with a refuge, a robust but fairly crude shelter, sometimes staffed, sometimes not, is that everybody sleeps together in a big dormitory – hardly hiding away. So, for a chance of having the place to yourself it helps to go in the low season. The very, very low season.

It isn't easy. Once we laboured up to the Sarradets Refuge at the Cirque de Gavarnie in a March snowstorm. At over 2,500 metres in those conditions and at that time of year we should have been guaranteed total and utterly utter privacy, yet we ended up spending two unromantic nights with a couple of skiers from the Massif Central who'd been given a bum forecast.

That having been said, a precious few mountain refuges actually have private rooms. Consult a good walking guidebook or put 'refuge' into your search engine together with the name of the destination.

*

With the name La Montaña Mágica, inspired by Thomas Mann's novel, it just can't be ignored. At Cuanda, near the village of El Allende, and only 10 km from the beaches at Llanes, La Montaña Magica is a collection of farm buildings lovingly restored and modernised (**www.helicon.es/cuanda.htm** Tel: 00 34 98 592 5176). Of the 14 double bedrooms, 10 have massage baths and six have a fireplace. The farmstead isn't very high but it has views of the Naranjo de Bulnes in the Picos de Europa.

*

California has some of the most beautiful and spectacular mountains in the world. In 1869 John Muir, a prime mover in the creation of Yosemite National Park and founder of the Sierra Club, worked as a shepherd in the Sierra Nevada. Forty years later he took out his notes and fashioned them into a book that has become a classic of mountain literature, *My First Summer In The Sierra*. Amazingly, there are places in a better state now than they were then, due to their protected sheep free status. His bed was mostly *'magnifica* fir plumes'. Yours will be somewhat different. Unfortunately, you won't be able to stay in the kinds of places John Muir did. The protection of mountains comes at a price, which is that everything is squashed together on the valley floor. Still, here and there are cabins that are a little more away from it than others. Take a look, for example, at **www.vrbo.com/38212** (Tel: 00 1 559 846 6539). Among the hotels, Yosemite Lodge has one of the best situations while the Wawone Hotel is one of the most curious with its period verandas looking something like a Mississippi river boat. For all accommodation inside Yosemite see **www.nationalparkreservations.com** (Tel: 00 1 406 862 8190). Once you've hiked away from the valley floor you'll be mighty pleased no development has been allowed to disturb the Sierra where, as Muir put it, "God himself is preaching his sublimest water and stone sermons."

Further information

Put 'mountain holidays' into your search engine together with the name of the destination. In the USA **http://totalescape.com** will find you a Forest Service cabin; also see **www.reserveamerica.com**.

Some specialist operators

www.crystallakes.co.uk Tel: 0870 888 0252
www.highmountain.co.uk Tel: 01993 775 540
www.allmountainholidays.com Online booking
www.austriatravel.co.uk Tel: 01708 222 000
www.lakes-mountains.co.uk Tel: 01329 844 405
www.peakretreats.co.uk Tel: 0870 770 0407

www.white-peak.com Tel: 0870 068 8047

Yosemite
www.archersdirect.co.uk Tel: 0870 460 3894
www.justamerica.co.uk Tel: 01730 266 588
www.virginholidays.co.uk Tel: 0870 220 2788
www.completenorthamerica.co.uk Tel: 0115 950 4555

Some questions to ask

✓ What's the altitude?
✓ What will the temperatures be in the daytime? At night?
✓ Will there be snow?
✓ What sort of footwear/clothing should I have?
✓ Is there central heating?

For a refuge
✓ Are there any private rooms?
✓ Is the refuge likely to be full?
✓ Will it be possible to have a meal?
✓ Is there electricity?
✓ Should I bring a sleeping bag?
✓ If I have only a sleeping bag liner will there be blankets?

Who are mountain holidays for?

Lovers of the outdoors; those seeking tranquillity, spirituality and, perhaps, adventure.

Pros

• You feel healthy just being there.

Cons

• Mountain weather is unreliable and sometimes unpleasant.

Where to go

France: Alps, Pyrenees. Spain: Pyrenees, Cantabrian Mountains/Picos de Europa, Sierra de Gredos, Sierra Nevada. Italy: Alps, Abruzzi. Greece: Pindus Mountains. California: Sierra Nevada.

When

The summer is too hot to tackle the mountains with the vigour they require. So, unless you just want to take it easy, spring is good and autumn is best (least snow).

Price guide

A fully inclusive seven day holiday to Europe's mountains will cost from around £500. You can double that for California's Sierra Nevada. The cheapest way is a no-frills airline, a backpack and nights spent in *gîtes* and refuges. The Hotel Bellevue costs around £50 per person b&b while Hotel Pilatus is around £30. La Montaña Magica costs around £50 a night for a double room.

Unusual Holiday No. 6: In The Desert

You don't have to go to the Middle East or the Sahara to experience desert. No further, in fact, than just behind the beaches of the Costa del Sol. You thought *A Fistful of Dollars* was filmed in Arizona? Wrong. It was filmed right here. *Lawrence of Arabia?* Right here (well, some of it). Just 20 km or so north of Almería, El Desierto de Tabernas extends for 11,625 hectares and most of it looks like Butch and Sundance should be coming round the corner any minute. In fact, the whole stretch of coast from Cabo de Gata north as far as Cartagena is backed by the sort of scenery that would make a camel smile.

After filming *Lawrence of Arabia*, the director David Lean built a beach house not far away on the coast at Carboneras while his location manager Eddie Fowlie built a hotel which he called El Dorado. At the time it was more or less a secret known only to those who worked in the film industry. Unfortunately, time has moved on. Carboneras is now a bustling resort and the El Dorado has become what is known as a 'boutique' hotel. But, for a few dollars more, you might like to try out a place that has hosted quite a few famous names (**www.eldorado-carboneras.com/english** Tel: 00 34 950 454 050).

The film sets have now become two theme parks called Mini Hollywood and Texas Hollywood, with a zoo and the usual bank hold-up twice a day. But none of the tourists stray any further and with a small rucksack and plenty of water you can enjoy as much solitude as you want. Two tranquil hotels on the fringes of the area (there are none in the desert) and not far from the sea are Finca Listonero, Cortijo Grande at Turre (Tel: 00 34 950 479 094) and Cortijo El Sotillo, San José (Tel: 00 34 950 611 100).

Tabernas isn't the only desert in Spain. (In fact, the whole place will be a desert pretty soon if nothing is done about global warming.) Las Bardenas Reales, just south of Pamplona, looks exactly like *The Badlands*, while Tenerife, Lanzarote, Gran Canaria and Fuerteventura all have enough sand (inland) to rebuild Madrid. For the deserts of Tenerife you may like to stay at the Parador de Canadas el Teide (see Up A Mountain above). In the Bardenas a suitably atmospheric sort of place to stay is Cuevas Ruben & Anabel, two caves in Valtierra (**www.lasbardenas.com** Tel: 00 34 948 830 063/00 34 661 846 757).

*

One of the world's greatest desert experiences lies in the south-eastern corner of California (and parts of Nevada, Arizona and Utah). Here the Mojave covers an area of 25,000 square miles, roughly equal to the size of Ireland. Within it are four parks of which the most famous is Death Valley National Park, which sets several American records. The record lowest is 282 feet below sea level (near Badwater) while the record highest temperature is 134°F (in 1913).

So Death Valley is best avoided in the summer. It was given its name by those who crossed to seek their fortunes in the California gold rush of 1849, following James Marshall's discovery of nuggets near Coloma the previous year. Quite a few didn't make it. If you're fascinated by that, you might like to attend the 49ers' annual encampment which takes place the second weekend in November (sing alongs, square dances, backcountry tours and more). Although, if you do, you won't exactly be getting away from people.

About $2 billion in gold was taken out of the ground before mining more or less ceased – but, who knows, you might find something that was overlooked.

It's in the nature of deserts that they aren't easy place to live. Or even run a hotel. In Death Valley it's a choice between the inexpensive Stovepipe Wells Village (**www.stovepipewells.com** Tel: 00 1 760 786 2387) the quite expensive Furnace Creek Ranch and the very expensive Furnace Creek Inn (both on **www.furnacecreek resort.com** Tel: 00 1 760 786 2345). For a bit more atmosphere Green Acres Ranch cabins, in the section of the Mojave close to Joshua Tree National Park, are just right (**www.thegreenacres ranch.com** Tel: 00 1 760 641 1044).

Wilderness camping (or what the Americans call 'primitive camping') is permitted in some areas of Death Valley (after obtaining a permit from the Visitor Center). For the less adventurous there are nine organised sites of various sizes. In Anza-Borrego Desert State Park you can camp anywhere.

Further information

For more information on the Bardenas look at **www.turismorural bardenas.com**, **www.toprural.com**, **www.tudelabardenas.com** and **www.bardenaactiva.com**. For the Mojave and Death Valley see **www.desertusa.com** and **http://mojave.californiahotels.com**.

Some specialist operators

www.naturalist.co.uk Tel: 01305 267 994 Tabernas
www.completenorthamerica.co.uk Tel: 0115 950 4555 Death Valley

Some questions to ask

✔ Where can I stay in the desert?
✔ What will the temperature be in the daytime? At night?
✔ Are the rooms air conditioned?
✔ Will I need any special equipment or clothing?
✔ Will there be any natural springs for water?

Who are desert holidays for?

The adventurous, the curious and, above all, the fit.

Pros

- If you really want to get away then you'll succeed.
- Deserts have a very special beauty.

Cons

- Some desert areas are nevertheless pretty popular with day trippers from the nearest holiday resorts.
- Conditions can be harsh.

Where to go

Anywhere in the Mojave Desert, California; the Spanish interior from Cabo de Gata north as far as Cartagena; the Canary Islands.

When

Depends. Death Valley temperatures are, well, deathly in the summer and can still be as high as 120°F in October. November is the start of the peak season but spring is the best bet – February to April, when the desert comes alive with flowers. Spanish desert is much less extreme but, even so, if you want to do more than plod lethargically around avoid July/August.

Price guide

With a no-frills airfare or a package to the Costa del Sol you could be experiencing desert for well under £500 for a week. For California you'll need to budget over £1,000 for a week. Green Acres Ranch cabins cost around £650 for a week for up to four guests.

Unusual Holiday No. 7: Bogs, Marshes And Swamps

If you want not merely to get away from it all but actually to disappear then Dartmoor is the place, specifically Fox Tor Mire. Conan Doyle gave it the name Grimpen Mire and featured it in *The Hound of the Baskervilles*. They say the only escapee from Dartmoor Prison who was never recaptured was seen heading in its direction. A more pleasant way to drop out of sight is to book into nearby Bovey Castle (**www.boveycastle.com** Tel: 01647 445 016), originally a private house and sporting estate in grand 1920s style and now the sort of hotel where you'd expect to bump into Sherlock Holmes.

The Gaelic name for Lewis is Leodhas meaning 'marshy'. Very apt. Most of it is covered by peat, up to 13 feet deep in places, and the interior is a bare and squelchy blanket bog where, in your wellies, you need never see another human being. There are hotels on the coast but your tranquillity will be better protected by staying in a croft type place. Try **www.kabois.co.uk** Tel: 07831 274 595 or **www.dalmoreholidays.com** Tel: 01561 340 636. On the west coast near the Calanais Standing Stones a tiny little hamlet has been marvellously restored with thatched roofs and dry stone (**www.gearranan.com** Tel: 01851 643 416).

Florida has more swamps and marshes than any other US state except Alaska. Really *swampy* swamps. Even today, after drainage, a third of Florida is still covered by cypress domes, wet prairies, mangrove swamps, sawgrass glades, pitcher plant savannahs and other wetlands. Lurking somewhere in all of that are black bears and panthers. Some of the wetlands are salt, some brackish and others fresh, created by hundreds of springs. There are campgrounds and cabins out there but very little in the way of what you might call a hotel. Fortunately a man by the name of Edward Ball built himself a lodge on Wakulla Springs in 1937. It was here they filmed *Creature From The Black Lagoon*. Now Mr Ball was a very wealthy man so it was a very big lodge. On the other hand, as a hotel, which it now is, it's rather small. Just 27 rooms. They're rather creaky by modern standards but as a guest you get to stay right in the middle of this 6,000 acre protected area when all the day visitors have gone. At night you'll hear crickets, frogs, owls, the bellowing of alligators and the calls of the black-crowned night-herons. You won't be able to drown them out with the TV – the rooms don't have any (**www.floridastateparks.org/wakullasprings** Tel: 00 1 850 224 5950).

Further information

For details of Florida's wetlands see **www.visitflorida.com** and for its most famous bog **http://everglades-national-park.com**. Florida's largest national forest and most serious wilderness is the Apalachicola – sinkholes, blackwater streams, swamps, *everything*.

Some questions to ask

✔ Is it possible to walk around?
✔ Are there boardwalks?
✔ Are there any dangerous beasties – snakes, spiders, alligators etc?
✔ What precautions should I take against mosquitoes?
✔ Is there anywhere to stay?

Who are bog holidays for?

Dedicated environmentalists.

Pros

● Marshland isn't popular so it's easy to find some to yourself.

Cons

● Messy, full of mosquitoes and difficult to walk in.

Where to go

Dartmoor; much of the Highlands and Islands; Florida.

When

Summer.

Price guide

A croft will cost around £300 a week for four. Wakulla Springs costs around £60 per room per night.

Unusual Holiday No. 8: Staying In A Monastery

In the days before tourism had ever been thought of, religious orders of various kinds were building in some of the world's most spectacular and beautiful places. Many were up mountains, where permission for a hotel would never be given today, while others were on remote islands. Saint-Honorat, just off Cannes, is one of those islands. Incredibly, even now, nothing has been built there other than the (admittedly, quite large) Abbaye De Lerins. The monastery was recently granted a monopoly on day trippers, cutting numbers from 60,000 to 20,000 a year, which is a good thing for anyone seeking inner peace, whether monk or sun worshipper.

The trick is to be able to stay behind when all the day trippers have gone. That privilege is in the hands of Brother Pierre-Marie, to whom you'll have to write, saying why you should be allowed to stay (clue: don't mention the all over suntan). If the Brother agrees, you can stay for from one to seven days in return for about £35 a night and a little help with tending the vineyards and gardens or cleaning. Like the monks you might want to get up at 4.30 am but it isn't obligatory. And you *will* have time for sunbathing. Write to Brother Pierre-Marie, Frère Hôtelier, Abbaye Notre Dame de Lérins, BP 157, 06406 Cannes cedex, France; further information **www.abbayedelerins. com** Tel: 00 33 4 92 995 420.

Unlike the broad-minded Brother Pierre-Marie the monks of Mount Áthos (in Greek Ayiou Oros or Holy Mount) don't allow women – and that includes farm animals. Quite a lot of men might say: *So what's the point of going?* Well, the point is that the 20 monasteries plus smaller hermitages occupy a staggeringly beautiful peninsula that is an autonomous and unspoiled part of Greece. Not only that, the number of visitors is restricted by a permit system to 100 men per day. Think about it. Where else could you truly get away from it all – no hotels, no beach bars, no discos – *beside the Mediterranean*? Those lonely, pine scented trails. The quiet little coves. You'll need to get a letter of recommendation from the British Embassy in Athens or the Consulate in Thessaloníki and then take that to the Greek Foreign Ministry in Athens (Administrative Division of Church Affairs) or the Ministry of Northern Greece in Thessaloníki (Administration of Foreign Affairs). A few days before the planned visit (longer in summer) you'll have to telephone to make a booking (00 30 2310 252 578). Sleeping is usually in dormitories. Don't miss the so-called hanging monasteries of Dhionisíou, Osíou Grigoríou and Símonos Pétra.

Greece has another slightly less famous but even more spectacular collection of monasteries known as the Metéora which means 'rocks in the air'. Situated near Kalambáka in Thessaly they were featured in the James Bond film *For Your Eyes Only*. Just visiting is difficult enough, given the precipitous steps (in the old days you'd have been winched up in a net). Try the Pension Arsenis, Metéora (**www.arsenis-meteora.gr** Tel: 00 30 243 202 3500).

Italy is probably the best country in Europe for a monastery based tour. They're not only in secluded locations in the countryside but also at some of the most central and prestigious addresses in the most important cities – in the heart of Rome, for example, as well as Venice, Florence, Assisi, Siena and Naples. Some are extremely beautiful with impressive art collections. If you're not a particularly religious person it's best to look out for a *casa religiosa* that has a *foresterie* or guesthouse. Here things will be relatively relaxed, couples will be able to sleep together and the curfew hour (most have them) will be appropriately late. For the stricter establishments you might need a letter of recommendation and be compelled to go to bed both early and alone. (*Not much fun, then. PJ*) The Casa di Santa Brigida close to the Piazza Farnese in Rome, a well known *foresterie,* has very comfortable rooms (with bathrooms), no curfew and no problem with couples (**www.brigidine.org** Tel: 00 39 06 6889). Others in Rome include Fraterna Domus, Casa di Santa Francesca Romana and the Centro Diffusione Spiritualità. In Venice you might like to try the Istituto San Giuseppe (Tel: 00 39 041 522 5352; around £35), a convent between Rialto and San Marco where all the rooms have private bathrooms.

Quite a few monasteries have been converted into real and rather impressive hotels. Villa Lupis, built by Camaldolite monks in the 11th century, is now an elegant base for exploring the area around Venice (35 miles), while Relais della Rovere in Tuscany was once the home of Pope Julius II. It was he who commissioned

Michelangelo to paint the Sistine Chapel, so he should have known a thing or two about interior decorating (**www.go-to-italy.com**). In the Spanish Pyrenees, Núria was a religious sanctuary and at 2,000 metres can still only be reached on foot or by rack railway (*cremallera*) from Ribes de Freser. So you certainly won't be bothered by traffic. The old *Santuario de Nuestra Señora de Núria* isn't what you'd call picturesque (a bit of a barracks, actually) but the three star Vall de Nuria Hotel inside is a lot better than a monk's cell (**www.valldenuria.com** Tel: 00 34 972 732 030).

Further information

Try putting 'monastery accommodation' into your search engine together with the name of the destination. If you're interested in Italy go to **www.initaly.com** for an abbreviated list of monasteries and convents; for the full list you'll have to pay 6 Euros. At **www.go-to-italy.com** you can reserve hotels that were former monasteries (such as the Villa Domus, Villa Vaticana and Villa del Foro, all in Rome).

Also try **http://goitaly.about.com**. For Greece see **www.gnto.gr** and then click on 'religious monuments'.

Some other monastery experiences

Kagyu Samye Ling Monastery, Scotland **www.samyeling.org** Tel: 01387 373 232 ext 22

Abbey of St Sixtus, Westvleteren, Belgium **www.sintsixtus.be** Tel: 00 32 57 401 970

Prince Of Peace Abbey, Oceanside, California **www.princeofpeaceabbey.org** Tel: 00 1 760 967 4200 ext 248

Who are monastery holidays for?

Believers and those who simply want to experience beautiful places unspoilt by commercialisation. Strong religious feeling isn't necessary in many cases – but it helps when the beds are hard and you have to get up at 4 a.m. for Matins.

Pros

- Access to places that are closed to ordinary tourists.
- A real opportunity to *think*, especially in those monasteries where talking is forbidden.

Cons

- Rules in some monasteries include no mobile phones, no loud conversations and no raucous laughter. (*Fat chance if there's a ban on couples. CS*)

Where to go

Mostly Italy and Greece.

When

Any time if you're mostly interested in the religious aspect; summer if you're more attracted by outdoor activities.

Price guide

Some monasteries have a set price. Others 'suggest' a 'donation' a little less than comparable accommodation in the world outside. In either case you're unlikely to pay more than £40 a night including meals and some (such as Samye Ling) are much cheaper.

Unusual Holiday No. 9: Hidden And Secret Places

It isn't always necessary to climb a mountain, sweat across a desert or squelch through a bog to find a quiet place to stay. Sometimes the best place to hide something is the last place anybody would look. So it can be with a hotel, guesthouse or cottage. It could be in the countryside, on the outskirts of a town or even in the middle of a capital city. The essentials are tranquillity and the ability to delight.

Further information

Nowadays quite a lot of operators are advertising 'hidden' locations and 'secret' places. Well, it all depends exactly what you mean by a secret. In Britain try **www.seclusionholidays.co.uk** and

www.countrycottagesonline.net. For the Continent **www.silence
hotel.com** Tel: 00 33 1 44 49 90 00; **www.secretplaces.com** Tel: 00 35
121 464 7430; **www.secretdestinations.com** Tel: 0845 612 9000;
www.paradores-spain.es; **www.pousadasofportugal.com**;
www.hiddenitaly.com Tel: 0800 10 77 822.

Some secret places

UK

www.thecitadelweston.co.uk Tel: 01630 685 204 The Citadel, North
Shropshire

Ireland

www.ardtarmon.com Tel: 00 353 071 916 3156 Ardtarmon House, Sligo

France

www.hotelpergolese.com Tel: 00 33 1 53 64 04 04 Hotel Pergolese,
Paris

www.lerelaisdutouron.com Tel: 00 33 553 281 670 Le Relais du
Touron, Dordogne

www.thefarmhouse.co.uk Tel: 00 33 4 50 79 08 26 The Farmhouse,
Morzine

Belgium

www.hotel-sandt.be Tel: 00 32 3 232 9390 'T Sandt, Zand, Antwerp

Netherlands

www.canalhouse.ne Tel: 00 31 20 622 5182 Hotel Canal House,
Amsterdam

Germany

www.hotel-advokat.de Tel: 00 49 89 21 63 Advokat, Munich

www.gastwerk-hotel.de Tel: 00 49 40 890 62 44 Hotel Gastwerk,
Hamburg

Spain

www.andalucia.com/accommodation/lossibileys/home.htm Tel: 626
955346 Hacienda Los Sibileys, Murcia

www.rocamador.com Tel: 00 34 924 489 000 Rocamador, Almendral

www.teleline.terra.es/personal/loslobos Tel: 00 34 956 640 429
Rancho Los Lobos, Jimena de la Frontera

www.mendigoikoa.com Tel: 00 34 94 6820 833 Mendi Goikoa, Axpe-
Atxondo

Portugal
www.saosat.com Tel: 00 351 21 928 3192 Convento São Saturnino,
Azoia, near Sintra

www.pousadasofportugal.com Tel: 00 351 275 980 050 Hotel Pousada
Sao Lourenco, near Manteigas

www.pousadasofportugal.com Tel: 00 351 245 997 210 Hotel Pousada
Flor de Rosa, Crato

Italy
www.borgoargenina.com Tel: 00 39 0577 747 117 Borgo Argenina,
Gaiole, Siena, Tuscany

www.villa-albarea.com Tel: 00 39 041 5100 933 Villa Albarea, Pianiga-
Venezia

www.bebvetan.it Tel: 00 39 0165 908 970 Petit Coin de Paradis, Vetan
Village

Greece
www.travel-to-arachova.com Tel: 00 30 2267 031 230 Santa Marina
Arachova, Mount Parnassus

Florida
www.alexanderhomestead.com Tel: 00 1 904 826 4147 Alexander
Homestead, St Augustine

California
www.wharfmasters.com Tel: 00 1 707 882 3171 Wharfmasters,
Mendocino Coast

www.standardhotel.com Tel: 00 1 323 650 9090. The Standard,
Hollywood.

And finally

A French TV station made a programme about a little place at 1,500 metres in the eastern Pyrenees called Mantet, describing it as 'the village at the end of the world'. It was. We know. We used to live there and, believe us, you'll never find another place like it this side of the Himalayas. Rent a house for up to 20 (**http://girada.free.fr** Tel: 00 33 4 68 05 68 69), stay at the *gîte* (**www.balades-pyrenees.com/gite_de_mantet.htm** Tel: 00 33 4 68 05 60 99) or take a room in the Auberge Le Bouf'tic (Tel: 00 33 4 68 05 51 76).

Other Hideaway Holidays: Chapter 1, Castaway Holidays; Chapter 3: Holidays With Animals; Chapter 6: Mind, Body And Spirit Holidays; Chapter 7: Extreme Holidays; Chapter 12: Snow Ball Holidays.

Chapter 3

Holidays with Animals

Unusual holidays in this chapter: horse riding, gypsy caravans, donkeys, manatees, dolphins, falconry, farm holidays, animal sanctuaries and much more.

Being around animals is relaxing. It's scientifically proven. So if you're going on holiday to destress, what better way than to go where there are horses to ride on and little furry animals to cuddle? Mind you, animals aren't so relaxing when they won't do what you tell them. (Which, come to think of it, can be quite a lot of the time.)

Unusual Holiday No. 10: Horsing Around

Nothing can beat being on horseback – except, perhaps, getting off again at the end of a long day's ride. Somehow the horse acts as a kind of bridge between you and nature (at least, once you've relaxed enough to look around). As Winston Churchill put it, something about the outside of a horse is good for the inside of a person. Forget just lying on the beach. Ponder, instead, cruising along it in an open-top sports job... with one horse power. Or, come to that, being carried to the tops of spectacular mountains or ambling through woods while deer bound ahead of you.

Don't go thinking this is only for 'horsey' people with thighs like nutcrackers. There are outfits that will take beginners. On the other hand, it doesn't makes sense to book a one or two week holiday without being sure you like horses. So, if you're attracted by the idea, arrange a few 'hacks' with a local stable first or, better still, different stables, so you experience various horses and styles.

Once you get comfortable with the idea that, unlike a car, you can only make a horse stop or turn right *if it wants to*, you're well on your way. (In fact, on a beginners' trek you'll find your horse will takes its cues from the guide's horse, anyway.) We began riding in the 'classical' style (the 'normal' way, if you like) but after a few years switched to Western. It suits *us*. It may not suit you. Try to find out.

The ingredients that really make a riding holiday aren't easy to find out till you get there. A sympathetic and companionable instructor is worth more than all the paper qualifications that exist, beautiful riding country is worth more than a luxurious club-house and a good horse with an old saddle is worth infinitely more than the finest tack money can buy.

Most riding holidays are based at a centre from which you set out every day. Accommodation (where available) is often fairly basic so, if you need a little luxury be sure to check carefully what's on offer or make your own arrangements with a convenient hotel. At the other extreme are the long distance treks – a week or more – camping in tents carried by pack horses. Just behind the Costa Brava, the Pyrenees are excellent for that. Some outfits, such as Chevaux de la Tramontane (**www.chevauxdelatramontane.com** Tel: 00 33 4 68 041 798) offer the chance to ride the whole range from the Atlantic to the Mediterranean, or stages in between.

Remember the key to a good riding holiday is a good horse. Don't get saddled with a mount that doesn't suit you (too wide, too volatile, too nervous, too slow…). Ask for a different one.

*

Ever since we watched the film *Dances With Wolves* we've wanted to see the buffalo herds of the Great Plains and ride amongst them. (*'Near them' will do for me. CS*) Then we discovered we didn't have to go anything like as far. No further, in fact, than the fringes of the beautiful Parc National de Cévennes in France where, at Lanuéjols, is a herd of more than 60 of the magnificent Randals Bison as well as Texas Longhorn (**www.randals-bison.com** Tel: 00

33 4 67 82 73 74). Accommodation is in dormitories and, for the ten-derfeet, a log built bunkhouse. No beginners on this one, but the number of 'ranches' in France is growing and others may have a different policy; take a look at the website for the French Western riding magazine: **www.equiwest-magazine.com** So it's, 'Head 'em up, move 'em out.'

*

At Rainbow Ranch, just behind the Costa Brava, you can choose a horse, feed it, brush it, care for it and generally hang around with it, a blade of grass dangling carelessly from your mouth, until you feel good and ready to ride. Rainbow Ranch is a centre for *equitherapy*, which recognises the Arab saying: the horse is your mirror. In other words, the horse reflects your inner world and until you feel comfortable with the horse, the horse won't feel comfortable with you. Equitherapy is so powerful it can even be used to treat quite serious psychological problems (in which case, clients have to be referred by a psychologist). We've seen some impressive – and quite moving – results. The centre is run by Reinard van Beek, a Dutchman, but he speaks perfect English (**www.rainbowranch.nl** Tel: 00 34 690 288 624). For other centres offering equitherapy get in touch with the Equine Assisted Growth And Learning Association **www.eagala. org.uk**.

*

If you love horses but can't quite afford a riding holiday then a working holiday could be the cheap answer. Fantasia Adventure Holidays based at Barbate on the Costa de la Luz has a limited number of working holidays available (**www.fantasiaadventure holidays.com** Tel: 00 34 956 431 609). That's a gift horse you certainly shouldn't look in the mouth. You'll have to assist the groom for two hours in the morning and two and a half hours in the evening, go on two to three full day rides a week and exercise horses that aren't working. Which, if you love horses, is what you'd want to do anyway. For other opportunities take a look at **www.payaway.co.uk**.

Further information

If you book through a specialist holiday operator the job of weeding out unsuitable stables is done for you and all arrangements taken care of. But if you prefer to book direct, which opens up a bigger range of choices, take a look at the listings and links on some of the specialist internet sites such as **www.equine-world.co.uk** or **www.equineseek.com** or **www.travel-quest.co.uk**. On your search engine try 'riding holidays' together with the name of the country. Another idea is to get hold of riding magazines from the country concerned. They'll have adverts and articles. Once you have a list of possibles, phone the stable and have a chat to get the feel of the place. But a recommendation from someone you trust is best of all.

Some specialist operators

www.inthesaddle.com Tel: 01299 272 997

www.equineadventures.co.uk Tel: 020 8667 9158

http://worldhorseriding.com Tel: 00 46 46 14 52 25 or 00 39 0363 301 434

www.hiddentrails.com Tel: 0870 134 4283

www.horserentals.com 00 1 877 446 7730

Some questions to ask

✔ What qualifications do your instructors have?

✔ Do you have horses suitable for my level?

✔ Will there be a good selection – in case I don't like the first horse I'm given?

✔ What style of tack do you use (eg 'classical' style, Western/cowboy style)?

✔ Do you own your horses or do you (this is best avoided) just rent them for the season?

✔ Is there a good variety of routes?

✔ What do I need to bring?

✔ Will I be insured?

Who are riding holidays for?

Anybody can learn to ride – and a horse is a great way of giving mobility to anyone with physical disabilities. A riding holiday can be great for families –

as long as the children are big enough to cope – because the shared experience really opens up communications.

Pros

- A great way of getting to know yourself – and the people you're with.

Cons

- Accommodation is seldom luxurious (although it can be).
- There's always an element of risk in being around horses.

Where to go

Wherever there are tourists there are horses but for really good trekking close to the usual holiday destinations try the Costa de la Luz, the Alpujarras just behind the Costa del Sol, the eastern Pyrenees just behind the Costa Brava/Côte de Vermeille and the Alentejo region beside the Portuguese Algarve. In California the Inyo National Forest is the place to relive the Old West, riding among the wild mustang herds – or maybe you'd prefer riding on the beach at Half Moon Bay, just south of San Francisco.

When

Riding is pretty miserable for horses and riders alike when it's very hot and there are masses of flies. In destinations like Spain or southern Portugal you'll be better off in the spring and autumn, or even winter. If you have to go in summer, stay north or choose somewhere high in, say, the Alps or Pyrenees.

Price guide

Herding bison costs around £80 a day, including meals and dormitory (£45 extra for private facilities). Rainbow Ranch charges £420-£840 per week for mobile homes for up to four people. Fantasia charges around £600-£700 for a week's riding holiday and the same for a *month's* working holiday.

Unusual Holiday No. 11: Putting A Horse Before A Cart

Who hasn't dreamed at some time of rolling slowly down a country lane in a pretty little caravan drawn by old Dobbin? Well, the idyll can easily be made to come true.

The traditional bow topped gypsy caravan is being made again, with modern fittings. Given the leisurely pace of travel – walking speed – the trick is to find somewhere with very little traffic and places to stop for the night every dozen miles or so (say, 20 km). In fact, they can be rented in all sorts of places, including the New Forest, the Brecon Beacons and the Pennines, but Ireland is really the home of this kind of travel. Typically, the caravans are laid out with a double bunk and two singles, plus cooking and washing facilities (but no toilet).

You don't need prior experience with horses, as long as you're a stable person. (*Groan*) A half day's tuition will sort all that out. A good operator will have a variety of routes and stopovers (very important) from which you can make your selection. If you think in terms of a half day on the move you'll have plenty of time for other things.

Further information

Try putting 'horse drawn' into your search engine or take a look at **www.travel-quest.co.uk** or **www.irishhorsedrawncaravans.com**.

Some questions to ask
✓ Can I also ride the carthorse?
✓ What things are there to do along the way?
✓ What facilities are available at stopovers?
✓ Will you come out and help us if we have a problem?
✓ Will we be insured against road accidents?

Who are horse drawn holidays for?
Romantic couples; families with medium sized children.

Pros

- A real stress buster.
- No previous experience with horses necessary.
- Less risky than sitting on a horse.

Cons

- Not so idyllic in the rain.
- You won't travel very far.

Where to go

Ireland.

When

Most companies operate only in the summer.

Price guide

This is an inexpensive holiday if there are four in the caravan. Think in terms of around £600 a week for the horse and caravan, plus £15 a night for a 'pitch', plus food and entertainment – and the cost of getting there.

Unusual Holiday No. 12: Travels With A Donkey And Others

If you don't like all the donkey work that goes with hiking then why not try, well, a donkey? That's how the writer Robert Louis Stevenson famously transported his picnic in *Travels With A Donkey In The Cévennes* and was made a bit of an ass of by his *âne* Modestine. Given the title of his book, the Cévennes – the hilly region behind the Languedoc beaches – is obviously the place to go. We know we've told you to 'ditch the donkey' but this is worth making an exception for. The idea is that you stroll along footpaths while the donkey carries your picnic and anything else you want – up to about 40 kg, which should be enough for the needs of about four people. Some operators can offer accommodation as well. Take a look at **www.volc-anes.com** for example (Tel: 00 33 4 73 85 84 12/00 33 6 07 03 63 09), based near St Gervais d'Auvergne, which offers two donkeys plus a *gîte* sleeping nine to 12.

But it's not only a donkey that can carry your picnic. A llama can, too. Try 'llama holidays' in your search engine or see **www. ukllamas.co.uk** for a trek with a difference in Dorset. On Lanzarote a camel will take you to the volcanoes of the Timanfaya National Park. You can even try a camel in Somerset (Bridgwater Camel Company Tel:01278 733 186).

Further information

Go to **www.ane-et-rando.com** and click on *où randonner?* for a list of operators all over France.

Some questions to ask

✓ As for Unusual Holiday No. 11 (see page 45).

Who are donkey holidays for?

Anyone frightened of actually sitting on a horse or being pulled along by one.

Pros

- Donkeys (and llamas) are really cute.
- Donkeys (and llamas) do… the donkey work.
- You'll never be short of funny anecdotes afterwards – because they're also stubborn.

Cons

- You'll get along much faster if you carry your picnic yourself.
- You might end up looking an ass.

Where to go

Anywhere around the French Massif Central for donkeys.

When

Summer.

Price guide

A donkey costs around £30 a day. The *gîte* at St Gervais d'Auvergne with two donkeys costs around £400 a week.

Unusual Holiday No. 13: Pat A Manatee And Other Nature Holidays

Several times dolphins have put on a show for us, dancing in the bow wave of our yacht. But never have we succeeded in swimming with them. A manatee, on the other hand, is an altogether different proposition. Manatees are the sloths of the underwater world. No way will these gentle monsters disappear at speed. When winter comes on in Florida (say, mid-October to the end of March) they gather at Crystal River where the water remains a pleasant 72°F year round. Amazingly, you can snorkel with them and just generally hang out. It gives a whole new meaning to: 'Hey, how you doin', Man?'

Put 'Crystal River manatee' into your search engine or take a look at **www.birdsunderwater.com**. Expect to pay around £20 for a three hour experience, plus the hire of snorkelling gear if you don't have your own.

For dolphins and whales a good place to start is **www.whaleguide. com** which gives links to a variety of tour operators. Not many people realise that nearly a third of the world's species of whales, dolphins and porpoises have been reported in Hebridean waters including, on occasion, the blue whale. If you don't mind heading a bit further north, say three hours from Heathrow, you'll increase your chances of blue whale to near certainty off Snaefellsnes, Iceland (**www.arctic-experience.co.uk** Tel: 01737 214 214).

One of the easiest places to see dolphins abroad is Gibraltar. Some 50 dolphins are resident but in summer numbers swell to several hundred, mostly common dolphins but also bottlenose and striped. The skippers who specialise in this can virtually guarantee an encounter. You can get a boat from Gibraltar itself or nearby Spanish resorts on the Costa del Sol and the Costa de la Luz. The secret of a profoundly moving experience is a small boat with no more than a dozen people – avoid the big ones. For an organised holiday try Wildlife Encounters (see specialist operators below) or make your own arrangements once there – see **www.gibraltar.gi/tourism** and click on 'dolphins'.

Twenty-eight species of dolphins and whales reside in or migrate through the waters south-west of la Gomera in the Canary Islands. The season is March to November but excluding June and the first half of July. You can make arrangements when you get there or book an inclusive package – take a look at the internet travel agency **www.responsibletravel.com**.

But the greatest place to see whales in the whole world is California, where commercial whale watching began in 1955 with Chuch Chamberlin's $1 boat trips. Winter is the time for grey whales and summer for blue whales, the biggest creatures that have ever lived on Earth, when several hundred gather in the Santa Barbara Channel. Take a look at the American Cetacean Society site **www.acsonline.org** for general information and try **www.montereybaywhalewatch.com** and **www.sanctuarycruises.com** for trips. Expect to pay around £60 for a full day. You can combine your California whale watching with visits to Yosemite (see Mountains above and **www.nps.gov/yose** and **www.yosemitepark.com**) for black bears, mule deer and bighorn sheep, while in the Mojave desert (**www.nps.gov/moja**) you might see mountain lion. You could also trek the John Muir Trail (see Chapter 4: Sport And Adventure Holidays).

If you like watching birds but can't really tell your *Anas*[1] from your eagle, then go for one of the big spectacles, such as the Col d'Orgambideska in the Pyrenees, through which some 22,000 migrating raptors pass each autumn, including short-toed and booted eagles, black and red kites, and honey and common buzzards. South Florida in the springtime will dazzle you with its nesting bald eagles, grey kingbirds, sandhill cranes, burrowing owls, red-cockaded woodpeckers and many others. Try **http://birding.about. com**, **www.fatbirder.com** or **www.birdforum. net**

---

[1] Anas platyrhynchos is the mallard

for links to specialist holiday companies as well as reports from birdwatchers about what's to be seen. Or buy one of the specialist magazines and check the adverts.

The 550 islands of the Hebrides are the finest places to see wildlife in all of the UK. On the island of Mull, for example, and in the surrounding waters and islets, you stand an excellent chance of seeing (among others) white-tailed sea eagles, golden eagles, ravens, puffins, otters, red deer, seals, porpoises and minke whales. For a fully organised holiday try Wildlife Encounters (around £500 for five nights – see panel). Or take a look at **www.wildlifemull.co.uk** for daytrips at around £30 or **www.isleofmullholidays.com** or simply put 'Mull wildlife holidays' into your search engine. If you'd like to help whales and dolphins in the Hebrides see 'Working Holidays' below.

Further information

Put 'nature holidays' into your search engine, or the name of the particular beast you want to see, together with the name of your destination.

Some specialist operators

www.naturalist.co.uk Tel: 01305 267 994
www.naturetrek.co.uk Tel: 01962 733 051
www.wildwings.co.uk Tel: 0117 965 8333
www.birdfinders.co.uk Tel: 01258 839 066
www.wildlife-encounters.co.uk Tel: 01737 218 802

Some questions to ask

✓ What birds and animals will I see?
✓ Is this going to be physically demanding?
✓ Is it suitable for children?
✓ What clothing and equipment will I need?

Who are nature holidays for?

Just about anybody interested in wildlife – but some holidays will require a reasonable degree of physical fitness.

Pros

- Getting back to nature restores perspective and develops the spirit (and, very often, the calf muscles, too).

Cons

- Can be tiring and uncomfortable.
- Going around in a group may not be your idea of watching wildlife (in which case, make your own arrangements with a personal guide).

Where to go

There are ibex to be seen behind the Côte d'Azur; mouflon not so far from the beaches of the Côte Vermeille; wild boar and bee eaters behind the Costa Brava; roe deer behind the Costa del Sol; dolphins around Gibraltar; whales and dolphins in the waters off the Canary Islands; 40 species of orchids and a third of all European species of butterflies within a short drive of the ferry terminal at Santander; one of Europe's most impressive colonies of huge griffon vultures not so far from the beaches of Biarritz; manatees in Florida and blue whales off the beaches of California. And that's just to start.

When

Depends what you want to see.

Price guide

Nature holidays tend to be relatively expensive because you have to pay for one or more specialist guides, plus (sometimes) off-road vehicles and boats – and the organising companies are usually quite small. In Europe, £1,000 for 10 days to a fortnight, all included, is quite normal. For an all inclusive nature holiday to California expect to pay twice that.

Unusual Holiday No. 14: A Bird In Your Hand

Imagine that, rather than seeing birds through field glasses, you could have, say, a barn owl or a kestrel or a peregrine falcon actually perched on your fist. Given a close up view of talons and hooked beaks you might feel apprehensive. But although the savage beauty of these birds is quite overwhelming they're perfectly docile with humans.

The way to do it is to book a *falconry* holiday. Quite a lot of places have sprung up that give what you might call 'flying demonstrations', but what you're looking for are serious courses with a maximum of three students per instructor. Any more is stressful for the birds, apart from which you just won't get to handle them very much.

The problem with falconry, for many people, is that it's a form of hunting. Of course, the bird is only behaving naturally but you may object to taking part in the killing of rabbits and pheasants. If you feel this way but would still like to get close to these raptors then book for the course minus the hunting trips. Afterwards, don't try any of what you've learned on your budgie at home.

Further information

You won't find falconry in ordinary travel brochures. Put 'falconry holidays' into your search engine or phone the tourist office where you'd like to go and ask what's on offer.

Some specialist operators

http://highlandfalconry.scotlandrocks.co.uk Tel: 01764 679 056
Mobile: 07739 036066

Some questions to ask

✓ How many students per falconer? (Avoid more than three.)
✓ What species of birds do you have?
✓ How much time will I have handling the birds?
✓ Can I opt out of the hunting?

Who are falconry holidays for?

Anyone who wants to get close to birds of prey (children are often accepted).

Pros

● Just about your best chance of interacting with raptors.

Cons

● Not for vegetarians, vegans or the squeamish.

Where to go

Lots of places, but Scotland and Exmoor are some of the best.

When

Any time, but check if you actually want to hunt.

Price guide

One day introductions cost in the region of £120 but for a five day course, covering all aspects of husbandry, expect to pay around £300. Your travel, accommodation and food will be on top.

Unusual Holiday No. 15: Working Holidays With Animals

A friend called one evening to say he had an eagle owl for release following veterinary attention. Apparently it had been shot – illegally – by a hunter but was now recovered.

This friend is an ornithologist who works for one of the parks in Spain. Naturally, we hurried round. No pictures or drawings had prepared us for the magnificence of the eagle owl, a female, close up. Awesome is the word that springs to mind. Every feather seemed to have been designed by a master couturier. Despite a beak like a scimitar she made no attempt to attack – this owl was a pussy cat. Handling her, and later releasing her, was an unforgettable experience. And it's the sort of experience you could also have on a working holiday with animals. Don't expect to get too cuddly, however, with the cetaceans that are the concern of the Hebridean Whale And Dolphin Trust (**www.hwdt.org** Tel: 01688 302 620).

Facilities on these kinds of holidays vary enormously, as do the prices – from the frankly expensive down to the very little – so take your time choosing. Some of the organisations concerned are simply delighted to have the help while, at the opposite extreme, others try to make a profit from working holidays (which all goes to help the cause). Accommodation and instruction are usually the only things included. You normally have to make your own travel arrangements and provide your own food. Sometimes you'll wonder if they really want you to come at all. Dedication helps. So not the most pampered of holidays – but, probably, the most memorable and usually for the right reasons.

Further information

Quite a large number of organisations now offer this kind of experience. Take a look at **www.support4learning.org.uk** for extensive links. For the USA try the national parks (**www.nps.gov/oia/topics/ivip.htm**) Read very carefully what's on offer and, if possible, speak to the person in charge on the ground. Don't leap at the first thing. Compare. Problems can arise over the contradiction between the words 'working' – what the charity or scientific body wants – and the word 'holiday', which is what you want. Be clear in your own mind what you're actually willing to do, how much free time you want and the standard of accommodation you're willing to accept.

Some specialist operators

www.wildwings.co.uk and click 'ecovolunteers' Tel: 0117 965 8333
www.earthrestorationservice.org Tel: 00 33 4 68 26 41 79
www.greenvol.com Tel: 01767 262 560
www.earthwatch.org Tel: 01865 318 831
www.btcv.org Tel: 01302 572 200
www.i-to-i.com Tel: 0870 333 2332

Some questions to ask

✓ Can I choose what work I do?
✓ Will I be working with the animals or doing something else?
✓ Will I have my own room?

✔ What is the average age of volunteers?

✔ How much free time will I have?

✔ Do I need any vaccinations?

Who are working with animals holidays for?

Most paying volunteers are under 25 so, if you're somewhat older, you might feel out of place. On the other hand, there's seldom an upper age limit as long as you're fit enough for the task.

Pros

- Contact with animals, if that's what you want.
- Instruction in techniques like tracking.

Cons

- Conditions can be basic.
- The work can be physically demanding.
- Some working holidays cost as much as normal holidays, or even more.

Where to go

Perhaps you'll be working with Iberian wolves at the sanctuary at Mafra in Portugal, monitoring monk seals at Karaburun in Turkey, ringing birds in Italy, counting whales off the Canary Islands or checking wild mustangs in California.

When

That entirely depends on the project.

Price guide

Prices vary enormously, depending on the policy of the organisation, the amount of instruction needed to be given and the costs involved in the work that's being done. The price, for accommodation only, could be as little as £100 a week working, for example, at an animal sanctuary. At the other end of the scale, on a high cost project like whale monitoring, the price could be as much as £750 for two weeks – with travel and food on top.

Unusual Holiday No. 16: Farm Holidays

Imagine being able to collect chicken's eggs for breakfast, help milk the cows, stroke the sheep, cuddle the rabbits, go riding, swimming, hiking and eat freshly picked vegetables for dinner. Then imagine coming back to a comfortable room with en suite facilities. Old MacDonald never had a farm like this!

Also imagine being able to go sightseeing, eating out and clubbing – because not every farm is in the 'middle of nowhere'. This is one of the great advantages of the farm holiday – you can usually find something to please everybody in a family or group, on the farm and in the surrounding area, provided you choose carefully.

Every farm is different. So be sure to ask exactly what's on offer and what the accommodation is like. Beware of the occasional, desperate farmer whose facilities really aren't up to the mark. Some organisations/websites have their own star ratings, just like hotels. In some cases it will be a room in the main farmhouse, in another a fully equipped apartment in the farmhouse and in yet another a completely self-contained cottage.

Further information

These aren't the kind of holidays that are normally found in brochures. You'll usually have to make your own arrangements. A good place to start tracking farms down is **www.agrisport.com** which gives links to 'tourism' farms all over the world. We're also giving you websites for specific countries.

Some specialist operators

www.farmstayuk.co.uk Tel: 024 7669 6909 UK

www.farmbreaks.org.uk UK

www.irishfarmholidays.com Tel: 00 353 61 400 700 Ireland

www.agriturismo.com Italy

www.bretagnealaferme.com Brittany, France

www.ecoturismorural.com Spain

www.bauernhof-ferien.ch Tel: 00 31 329 66 33 Switzerland

www.farmholidays.com Austria

www.tiscover.at Austria

www.farmholidays.de Germany

Some questions to ask

✔ What things are there to do on the farm?

✔ Will we be able to help with the animals?

✔ Is the accommodation self-contained or a room in the farmhouse?

✔ What things are there to do in the surrounding area?

✔ Is the farm within walking distance of a village/town?

✔ Will there be other holidaymakers staying on the farm?

Who are farm holidays for?

Great for families, groups of friends and nature lovers.

Pros

- Plenty of contact with domestic animals.
- Tranquillity (except when there are cocks crowing at 4 am).

Cons

- You might need your wellies to walk to the car.
- Some farms may be a long way from anywhere else.

Where to go

Austria is a delight for this type of holiday, with generally excellent facilities. In France the *ferme pedagogique* has long been established as a way of teaching schoolchildren about rural life. Other good bets are Ireland, Bavaria (Germany), Switzerland…and the UK.

When

Summer.

Price guide

These holidays are usually very good value. Expect to pay from as little as £150 for a two person apartment on the farm for a week – but with travel and food on top.

And finally

Why not take your own dog backpacking? You carry your load and he carries his. A mature dog in good condition can handle between a quarter and a third of its weight. Several manufacturers make packs especially for dogs. Put 'dog backpack' into your search engine or take a look at **www.canine-spirit.com**.

For backpacking elsewhere in the EU your dog will need a microchip, vaccination against rabies, an EU pet passport and – this is where advance planning is important – a blood test six months before the date you will return home. At the end of your holiday, your dog must be treated against ticks and tapeworm by a vet 24-48 hours before being checked in with your ferry, airline or train.

Full details: **www.defra.gov.uk/animalh/quarantine/pets/procedures/owners.htm**.

Other Holidays With Animals: Chapter 4: Sport And Adventure Holidays; Chapter 7: Extreme Holidays; Chapter 12: Snow Ball Holidays.

Chapter 4

Sport and Adventure Holidays

In this chapter: hiking, swimming, snorkelling, surfing, windsurfing, cycling and mountain biking, canoeing and sea kayaking, indoor climbing, golf, tennis and much more.

Holidays are a time for simply relaxing, for chilling out, for lying on the beach with a good book or even a bad one. Right? Wrong! That's bor-*ring*! Holidays are a time for having adventures, trying new things and exercising away the flab that accumulated at the office. Come *on*!

Unusual Holiday No. 17: Hiking

The idea of hiking day after day can seem pretty daunting, especially if wilderness camping is involved. How do you clean your teeth? Where do you plug your razor in? How do you, you know, go to the, er, toilet?

But it's all worth it. The sunrise from a mountain top, the shady path by the river, the swim in the lake, the ducks gliding down at sunset, the delicious fatigue at the day's end and the sense of accomplishment.

And, in fact, you really don't have to camp at all. That's just one way of doing it (the purist way). Another way is to stay in a centre (in as much luxury as you want or can afford) and make day walks in the surrounding area. A third possibility is to hike from hotel to hotel with your luggage transported by your tour operator.

If you haven't done any serious hiking before don't contemplate the more demanding routes without an experienced companion, a guide or the organisational skills of a specialist operator. If it's solitude you're seeking wait till you've first gained some experience.

Getting the equipment right is tricky. We'd hate to encourage anyone to be irresponsible. On the other hand, legions now set off for an afternoon stroll equipped for an Everest summit bid. The more you carry, the slower you go, the more likely you are to get caught out far from civilisation.

We have friends who are mountain guides and hear a lot of their stories. The client who, having arrived at a mountain refuge, wanted to know where he could plug in his electric razor. The group who said they were used to walking but all collapsed the first day and refused to go any further. Be realistic about your level of fitness and the degree of comfort you require.

Whole books are written on the art of backpacking and hiking so here we can't do more than give some basic guidelines. The first is to be fit before you go. In a one or two week holiday there just isn't the time to build up. If you're not fit you stand a greater risk of injury at the start. Don't bring brand new equipment – make sure everything has been tested and worn in on some hikes at home, especially boots (which might otherwise cause blisters). If you're going without a guide polish up your navigation skills and take with you maps, compass and, if you can afford it, GPS (if you haven't yet caught on to the global positioning system see **http://home.earthlink.net**). As to that question of how you, er, go to the toilet, take a small trowel with you. At the very least, dislodge a manageable boulder, use the depression underneath and replace it. Paper should be burnt *unless there's a fire risk* (as there is in most of the Mediterranean in the summer).

Further information

There is a huge number of helpful sites on the internet. A good place to start is the Ramblers Association **www.ramblers.org.uk** Tel: 020 7339 8500. Also take a look at **www.walkingpages.co.uk**, **www.traildatabase.org**, **www.walkingworld.com** and **www.hikingandbackpacking.com**. Try putting 'walking holidays' into your search engine, together with the destination that interests you. Useful magazines include *TGO (The Great Outdoors)* and *Country Walking*. Look out for the *Sunflower Landscapes* series of guides which specialises in hikes near popular beach resorts.

Some specialist operators

www.inntravel.co.uk Tel: 01653 617 722
www.waymarkholidays.com Tel: 01753 516 477
www.foottrails.co.uk Tel: 01747 861 851
www.ramblersholidays.co.uk Tel: 01707 331 133
www.contours.co.uk Tel: 01768 480 451

Some questions to ask

✔ What style of hiking is involved – day walks from a centre, walking from hotel to hotel with luggage transported ahead or walking in the wilderness and camping overnight?
✔ What facilities (electricity, private rooms, showers, toilets etc) will be available at the overnight stops?
✔ Is this suitable for youngsters?
✔ Do I need to be insured?
✔ What equipment should I bring?
✔ What sort of shoes/boots are appropriate?
✔ Can I rent equipment?
✔ How much will I need to carry?

What distance will we be covering each day – and how much ascent and descent? (If you're not used to mountains an ascent of 300m will add about an hour to walking time on the flat and 1,000m is as much as most people can manage in a day.)

Who are hiking holidays for?

A hiking holiday is something everybody should try at least once in their lives.

Pros

- You'll be incredibly fit by the end of your holiday.
- You'll probably lose weight.

Cons

- If you overdo it you could finish the holiday exhausted.
- Creepy crawlies.
- If your hiking itinerary involves camping or mountain refuges you're going to have to accept a degree of discomfort.

Where to go

The UK Lots of possibilities such as the South West Coast Path; the Pembrokeshire Coast Path; Offa's Dyke; the Great Glen Way; the Rob Roy Way.

Ireland The North-West Passage from Dublin to County Donegal; the Kerry Way and Beara Way on the 'five fingers'; the Wicklow Way; the Western Way.

France A total of 40,000 km (25,000 miles) of Grande Randonnée (GR) footpaths including the GR1, an easy 605 km circuit round Paris, beginning at the château of Sceaux which should take about three weeks; the GR10 Traverse of the Pyrenees from Hendaye to Banyuls-sur-Mer, a moderate to hard 700 km (also possible by the much more demanding 45 day Pyrenees High Level Route); the GR22-22B, an easy 288 km trek from Paris to Mont St Michel; the GR223 228 km coastal walk from Avranches to Cherbourg; the 841 km GR34 tour of Brittany.

Netherlands The Gelrepad among woods, lakes and beautiful countryside in eight stages beginning at Enschede.

Belgium The GR5A and E9, both of which take you through varied scenery along and near the coast; the *Transardennaise*, a 160 km route through the forests and meadows of the Ardennes.

Germany The Black Forest, with its 23,000 km of footpaths; the Harz and

Hochharz National Parks; the Wadden Sea.

Spain The Camino de Santiago, the famous pilgrim route running for 730 km from Roncesvalles to Santiago de Compostela (see also Chapter 6: Mind, Body And Spirit Holidays for more details); the GR11 Traverse of the Pyrenees from Cap de Creus to Irún in 38 stages.

Portugal The Montesinho Natural Park, home of the Iberian wolf.

Italy The Abruzzo; Tuscany; the Dolomites.

Greece Anywhere in the Pindos Mountains; you might like to have a go at Mount Olympus, at 2,917 metres the highest in Greece; on Crete the White Mountains and Samariá Gorge.

Turkey The Taurus Mountains and Lakeland.

USA In California it has to be the John Muir Trail, a distance of 211 miles from Yosemite Valley to Mount Whitney, passing through three national parks; in Florida the 1,400 mile Florida Trail.

When

There's nothing more miserable than a hiking holiday in the rain except, perhaps, a hiking holiday when it's incredibly hot. Summer is the only time for Scotland. The early autumn is best in the high southern mountains (the Alps, Pyrenees, California's Sierra Nevada etc.) Winter and spring can be ideal for low-level treks in the Mediterranean. Check the weather data very carefully for where you want to go.

Price guide

Hiking holidays can be very good value *once you've got the necessary equipment*. For going it alone in the wilderness, a good backpack, boots, tent, sleeping bag and all the ancillaries could easily set you back £1,000. On the other hand, if you're only day walking between hotels £200 should cover it. As to the holidays themselves, think in terms of around £500 a week all inclusive up to around £1,000 in high season.

Unusual Holiday No. 18: Cycling And Mountain Biking

On a bicycle you'll cover a lot more ground than you ever could on foot, which makes a bike an excellent way of exploring a region. On a flattish road the average person should have no trouble covering 30, 40 or even 50 miles a day. After all, in the *Tour de France* they polish that off in a couple of hours. Mind you, on the *Tour* they don't have any luggage. You do. So if you don't want to be wearing your cycling shorts for dinner a specialist operator who'll transport your black tie from hotel to hotel is worth paying for. *Cycling For Softies* was one of the first into this market 20 years ago and is still pedalling along (see below). We tested one of their holidays at the time, pottering about in the Beaujolais region from prebooked restaurant to prebooked restaurant and prebooked hotel to prebooked hotel. Very pleasant it was, too.

Mountain biking, on the other hand, is a completely different activity altogether. A mountain bike may look much like a 'softie' bike but the resemblance is entirely superficial. Mountain bikes are for whooshing down steep mountain trails strewn with boulders and loose rocks, leaving strips of skin behind you as you go. Of course, there's no law that says you have to do it that way. But people who sign up with specialist operators tend to want to. If that's not your thing, look for destinations with plenty of wide dirt tracks from which you can enjoy the scenery without feeling you've been inside a cement mixer.

It should be pointed out that good mountain bikes are horribly expensive. Around £100 will buy an acceptable road bike but an awful mountain bike. They can cost up to £3,000 and your enjoyment depends very much on having a superior model with some kind of suspension, otherwise you'll feel as if you're being shaken to pieces (especially your wrists). Something like six inches of 'travel' in the rear suspension is good. Naturally, this all adds to the total cost of a mountain biking holiday. Serious operators don't even include the cost of bike hire because some enthusiasts will want to bring their own while others will want to choose from a range. To give you an idea, a basic but nevertheless serious mountain bike will cost around £70 a week to rent while a top of the range model will be over £200. You gets what you pays for.

If you don't like sweating your way up mountains make sure there are working lifts before committing to a destination (the lift pass is usually extra).

Further information

The Cyclists Touring Club is a good place to start (**www.ctc.org.uk** Tel: 0870 873 0060) while for mountain biking the specialist body is the International Mountain Biking Association (**www.imba.com**). Other useful sites include **www.trailquest.co.uk**, **www.nwmba.demon.co.uk** (for Wales) and **www.hmba.org.uk** (for the Highlands). For tour operators put 'cycling holidays' or 'mountain bike holidays' into your search engine together with the name of your chosen destination.

Some specialist road bike operators

www.cycling-for-softies.co.uk Tel: 0161 248 8282
www.bicyclebeano.co.uk Tel: 01982 560 471
www.wideopenroad.co.uk Tel: 0797 457 2629
www.lifecycleadventures.com Tel: 0800 587 8663

Some specialist mountain bike operators

www.alpineelements.co.uk Tel: 0870 0111 360
www.trailbreak.co.uk Tel: 0118 976 2491
www.skedaddle.co.uk Tel: 0191 265 1110
www.roughtracks.com Tel: 07000 560 749
www.cycleactive.co.uk Tel: 01768 840 400
www.outbreak-adventure.com Booking online

Some questions to ask

✔ What quality of mountain bike are you supplying?
✔ Will it have suspension? In the front? In the rear?
✔ What happens if there's a breakdown or a puncture?
✔ Do you have back-up by 4WD vehicle?
✔ Is bike hire included in the price or extra?

✓ Are new parts for wear and tear included in the rental price?
✓ Can I bring my own bike?
✓ Is insurance included?

Who are cycling and mountain biking holidays for?

If you don't do any cycling at home mountain biking is unlikely to be for you. Cycling on dirt paths and tracks is harder work than on a road so you need to be fairly fit. That having been said, it's more enjoyable away from the traffic and you can make it as easy or as hard as you like.

Pros

- You'll get fit.
- You can cover a lot more ground than hiking.

Cons

- Hard work if you're really doing it in the mountains.
- Cyclists are a little vulnerable on mountain tracks, and *extremely* vulnerable on busy roads.

Where to go

On a road bike anywhere without traffic, especially the Highlands and Islands, Ireland, rural France, inland Spain and California's wine country. On a mountain bike the Lake District, Pennines, Quantocks, Brecon Beacons, Snowdonia and Scottish Highlands in the UK; the Alps, Jura, Cevennes and Pyrenees in France; the Picos de Europa, Pyrenees, Sierra de Gredos and Sierra Nevada in Spain; Sardinia; Marin County, Lake Tahoe's Rim Trail, Mammoth Mountain and Santa Cruz in California.

When

Spring and autumn are best when the weather isn't too hot and places not too busy (for mountain biking autumn especially because there can still be snow in the spring).

Price guide

Road bikes A week's gastronomic bike tour in Provence or the Luberon with *Cycling For Softies* costs over £1,000 in high season, excluding flights, but companies that put less emphasis on luxury have holidays for half that.

Mountain bikes A week's holiday in the Alps will cost from £350-£500 in basic accommodation, excluding flights. On top of that you'll have to pay from £70 up to more than £200 for the hire of a serious bike. For California you could pay as much as £2,000 for a 14 day mountain biking holiday.

Unusual Holiday No. 19: Swimming

Most people go swimming on holiday so what's unusual about that? Ah yes, but we're not talking about the occasional swim when you're there, we're talking about swimming *to get* there. Well, let's not exaggerate. But imagine starting out on one Greek island and swimming to your hotel on the next. Or doing the same in the Isles of Scilly. Or swimming the length of Königsee in Bavaria. Or swimming back to Europe from Asia across the Hellespont (see also Chapter 10: Romantic Holidays). These are some of the itineraries for keen swimmers on offer from SwimTrek (**www.swimtrek.com** Tel: 020 8696 6220). How keen is keen? Well, you don't have to be capable of hauling your luggage behind you – that's taken care of by the support boat. But you do have to be capable of daily averages of 3-5 km. Think in terms of around £350 for a weekender and £625 for six days.

If you can't swim very well but would like to, take a look at 'Sports Clinics' (below).

Unusual Holiday No. 20: Snorkelling

Water covers over 70 per cent of the Earth so if you haven't stuck your head under the surface you can't really say you've travelled very much.

And it really isn't difficult. All you need is a face mask, a snorkel, a pair of fins and a little pluck. Oh yes, and in most places a swimming costume. In cold waters you'll also need a wetsuit (and the appropriate weights, to counter its buoyancy) but not in the Mediterranean in summer.

A friend told us she quite liked snorkelling except, she complained, water kept getting into her snorkel. Well, *water is supposed to get into your snorkel*, as we'll explain in a moment. If, like our friend, you're not too keen on getting the sea in your mouth and ears and up your nose you could just swim along the surface, keeping the top of your snorkel well clear of the water and watching what's going on below. In the transparent waters of the Med you can already see a lot without diving down.

But if you want to get a bit closer to the amazing creatures under the sea, to say hello to the octopus or whatever it is face to face then, yes, obviously the water will go down your snorkel. Get used to the idea. When you surface you blow hard, like a dolphin, and clear the tube again. You're also going to have to learn how to clear your ears to stop them hurting (which they do at about 3 metres); how to expel water from your mask while you're beneath the surface; and, indeed, how you actually *get down* under the water (easy when you can't swim, harder when you can). In other words, snorkelling may not be difficult but it isn't simple either. You're going to need lessons.

The first time you'll feel you're suffocating after just a few seconds. But once you get more comfortable under water you'll easily manage half a minute and, with a little persistence, a full minute. Lots of people snorkel for the odd half-hour's respite from just lying on the beach. But that wouldn't be a *snorkelling holiday*. For that you need a place with plenty of underwater life, a book to identify what you see and an underwater camera to record it. The latter can come quite cheap in the throwaway variety.

What might you see? Well, first of all, the astonishing light show as the surface ripples break the sun's rays into fantastic patterns. Then a mind-boggling variety of life more diverse and closer than you'll ever observe on land – common and white spotted octopus, various corals, anemones, sea cucumbers, starfish, bizarre sea potatoes, eels, scorpionfish, venerable grouper, barracuda, colourful rainbow wrasse, the astonishing plate-shaped sunfish, jellyfish (*jellyfish! I'm outta here. CS*) ... It's endless. You could even get the chance to snorkel with dolphins, one of the greatest experiences in the world (see also Chapter 3: Holidays With Animals).

Further information

The best place to get started is your local branch of the British Sub-Aqua Club (**www.bsac.com** Tel: 0151 350 6200) or, on holiday, any diving school. Don't be put off by the fact that most people will be there to learn scuba. Explain that you just want to concentrate on snorkelling.

Some specialist operators

www.adventure-breaks.com Tel: 01437 781 117

www.activitiesabroad.com Tel: 01670 789 991

www.tallstories.co.uk Tel: 01932 252 002

www.adventure-sports.co.uk Tel: 01736 761 838 (winter);
020 8816 7711 (summer)

www.call2venture.co.uk Booking online

Who are snorkelling holidays for?

Anyone who gets bored on the beach or is just curious about what's going on in *the deep*. Once children can swim competently they can snorkel, too.

Pros

- It's healthy.
- You'll see how the other half live (well, seven-tenths actually).

Cons

- Some people get a bit claustrophobic under water.

Where to go

Rocky places have more life than sandy, and the visibility is better, too. In Britain you'll need a wetsuit to enjoy the Scottish Lochs and Islands, Pembrokeshire, Cornwall and the Isles of Scilly as you will Ireland. In the Mediterranean there's excellent snorkelling on the Costa Brava, the Balearics, the Canary Islands, Corsica, Sardinia, the Côte d'Azur, the Bay of Naples, Sicily, Linosa, Corfu, the Aegean...in fact, just about anywhere with a rocky coastline.

When

It's not a lot of fun when it's cold or storms have destroyed the visibility so June to October tends to be the season in the northern hemisphere (there's also more light when the sun is high in the sky).

Price guide

Your basic equipment will cost you from £50 up to £250 or even more if you want the very best. Otherwise, snorkelling will cost you the same as any other holiday by the sea.

Unusual Holiday No. 21: Surfing

We've all seen the stunning pictures of bronzed men and women crouched defiantly inside the sunlit barrels of breaking waves, but not many of us have done it. Which is a pity. Because surfing holidays can be cheap, fun and very sociable. How about a surf safari, for example, travelling all down the coast of Portugal with a group of like-minded people?

If you live in the London area a good way of testing the water, so to speak, is to get the *Big Friday Surf Bus* which all through the summer leaves London on Friday evening and returns Sunday evening, giving you a weekend in Newquay to have a go (**www.bigfriday.com** Tel: 01637 872 512). If you enjoy that then a full scale holiday could be for you.

As a beginner you'll want the stability of a 'longboard' or Malibu (about eight feet for an adult). Ideally it should be a soft board or 'foamie', which is highly buoyant and very forgiving. But once you've got the hang of things you'll graduate to a shorter 'pop-out' – surfer speak for a production line foam board covered with fibreglass.

The first big problem is standing up on the board – the 'pop-up'. As soon as you've 'caught' a wave (by paddling) you grab the rails (sides), straighten your arms (as if doing a press up) and bring your legs under your body. Speed and smoothness are essential. It helps to practise on the beach (or at home) before making a fool of yourself on the water. The second big problem is staying up – pretty tricky when there's no binding to hold you to the board.

Some people manage the pop-up the first day. If you still haven't managed it after three days but enjoy the sensations you might like to consider kneeboarding (ie you stay on your knees) or bodysurfing (ie you don't have a board at all).

Further information

For general information contact the British Surfing Association (**www.britsurf.co.uk** Tel: 01637 876 474). Other useful sites include **www.surfing-waves.com** and **www.surfingholidays. net**. For kneeboarding see **www.kneeboardsurfing.co.uk** and **www.kneelo.org**; for bodysurfing see **www.body-surfing.co.uk**. Useful magazines include *Wavelength*, *Carve*, *The Surfers Path* and especially *Coast* which is on DVD. For specialist operators try putting 'surfing holidays' into your search engine together with the name of the destination.

Some schools in the UK

Surfer's World, Devon (**www.surfersworld.co.uk** Tel: 01271 890 037)

Coast to Coast Adventure Sports, Scotland (**www.c2cadventure. com** Tel: 01368 869 734)

Ma Sime's Surf Hut, Wales (**www.masimes.co.uk** Tel: 01437 720 433)

Some specialist operators

www.purevacations.com Tel: 01227 264 264
www.surfspain.co.uk Tel: 01691 649 992
www.winterwaves.com Tel: 07734 681 377
www.atlanticriders.com Booking online
www.extremeholidays.com Tel: 0870 036 0360
www.adventurebug.com Tel: 00 34 952 894 308 or 00 34 635 817 819

Some questions to ask

✓ What type of board will I start on? (Complete beginners need soft boards or 'foamies'.)

✓ Is your school British Surfing Association approved?

✓ Will I be insured? (Third Party cover is essential.)

✓ How reliable is the surf?

✓ What height is the surf likely to be?

✓ How many pupils per instructor?

✓ What is the average age of your clients?

Who are surfing holidays for?

Normally the young but there's no reason oldies can't do it as well. Whatever your age you need to be a good swimmer.

Pros

- Youthful camaraderie.
- If you don't take to it you can still enjoy the beach.
- You don't have to buy a lift pass (as for skiing).

Cons

- Youthful camaraderie.

Where to go

In the UK North Cornwall is the best, especially Crooklets Beach, Widemouth Bay, Watergate Beach, Newquay, Perranporth, Gwithian and St Ives; also the Gower and Pembrokeshire. In Ireland head for Donegal Bay – in fact, the whole west coast is a paradise. In Europe this is one time you don't want the Med (no surf); go for Portugal and the west coast of Spain, Madeira (not beginners), Fuerteventura and Lanzarote (all year). Florida is unreliable but can have good surf during the cyclone season (August-October) and sometimes in winter – try Cocoa Beach and Sebastian Inlet. California is the Mecca – anywhere between Santa Cruz and Half Moon Bay.

When

Autumn – the surf is too small in summer and the water too cold in winter.

Price guide

Surfing holidays can be really cheap. A 'surf safari' in Portugal is £200-£300 a week including food and accommodation in tents (but not flights). At the other extreme, surfing based at a good hotel in California could cost £1,000 or more for a week. If you want to do your own thing, lessons should cost around £25-£40 a day, depending on the size of the group, and the hire of a wetsuit and board around £50 a week. You can buy your own beginner's board for around £200.

Unusual Holiday No. 22: Windsurfing And Dinghy Sailing

Windsurfing is something lots of people try once on holiday whereas for others it *is* the holiday. It gets them the way skiing does – they like to be out there all day, every day. You might be the same.

The first hours are pretty discouraging. And tiring. You're going to fall off a lot. Especially when you try to turn. And having to haul the hinged mast back up each time won't do much for your humour (although it will do wonders for your arms). But gradually you'll begin to get the knack. You'll start knowing how much to angle the mast, how much to let out the sail and how much to lean. Then comes the moment you tack (turn) for the first time without falling off. And suddenly you're hooked.

Or not. If not, maybe dinghy sailing is more your thing. At least you get to sit down, capsizing is far less frequent (though harder to recover from) and you generally have company. What's more, you actually get to go somewhere (an inaccessible beach perhaps) and can take something useful with you (such as a picnic). At first you may have to be part of a flotilla but, once you've proven yourself, you should be able to explore on your own.

Some people protest that any kind of sailing involves arcane mysteries that will always be beyond them but, in fact, it's all perfectly logical and very good fun.

Further information

For general information try the UK Windsurfing Association (**http://ukwindsurfing.com** Tel: 01273 454 654) or, for both windsurfing and dinghy sailing, the Royal Yachting Association (**www.rya.org.uk** Tel: 0845 345 0400/023 8060 4100). For links to a wide range of windsurfing operators take a look at **www.windsurfingholidays.net** or try putting 'windsurfing holidays' into your search engine together with the name of your chosen destination. For links to dinghy sailing holidays take a look at **www.jojaffa.com** or put 'dinghy holidays' into your search engine together with the name of your chosen destination.

Some specialist operators

www.planetwindsurf.com Tel: 0870 749 1959
www.crystalactive.co.uk Tel: 0870 402 0275
www.extremeholidays.com Tel: 0870 036 0360
www.sunsail.com Tel: 0870 777 0313
www.neilson.co.uk Tel: 0870 333 3356
www.adventurebug.com Tel: 00 34 952 894 308

Some questions to ask

✓ What is the pupil to instructor ratio?
✓ Will I be insured?
✓ Do you follow the RYA teaching guidelines (applies to both windsurfing and dinghies)?
✓ Are the winds reliable? What force?
✓ What kind of dinghies are available? (Wayfarers are good for families, Fireballs and 505s for two people, Toppers and one man Lasers for individualists.)
✓ What's the depth of the water? (For novice windsurfers it helps if you can stand up.)
✓ Will I be learning in an area reserved for windsurfers? (It's safer if there are no swimmers, paddlers etc.)

Who are windsurfing/dinghy sailing holidays for?

You need to be a fairly good swimmer and be in possession of considerable determination for windsurfing. It helps to be young but we've seen people in their seventies give it a go. Any moderately fit person can sail a dinghy.

Pros

- Exhilarating.
- You don't need surf.

Cons

- Gallons of ocean will be consumed before you're a competent wind-surfer (and some of it's not too clean).

Where to go

Anywhere there's water you can windsurf but, as a beginner, you ideally need a large expanse of calm, shallow water with constant wind. A lagoon is ideal, as, for example, on the Roussillon coast of France at Port-Leucate and Port-Barcarès. Tenerife, Sardinia, Kos, Corfu and Rhodes are all favourites. If you're good, or think you will be, Tarifa is considered to be the windsurfing capital of Europe, given its strong winds. For dinghy sailing you really need an interesting coastline or nearby islands that give you somewhere to go – the Cyclades and the Dodecanese are perfect.

When

Summer, unless you're crazy.

Price guide

All inclusive windsurfing/dinghy sailing holidays in the Med cost from around £500 a week to well over £1,000 in high season. Tuition is on top – a one day windsurfing course for beginners will cost around £45 after which you'll be ready to practise on your own. Or you could opt for a series of one hour lessons. If the windsurf isn't included you'll have to pay another £120 or so a week to hire one, rather more for a dinghy.

Unusual Holiday No. 23: Canoeing And Sea Kayaking

The wonderful thing about river canoes and sea kayaks is the sense of being part of the environment. You make no noise, cause no pollution, see wildlife others miss and get to places larger craft just can't reach. Rivers come in two categories. Fast and foamy or placid and peaceful. Most holidaymakers opt for the latter. The great advantage of a river over the sea, of course, is that it does most of the work for you. With just the occasional dip of a paddle to keep you on course, villages, castles, restaurants, vineyards, weeping willows and gorges come gliding past. Some operators organise your overnight stops for you. All you have to do is float along until you come to the next hotel.

In the sea, on the other hand, a kayak doesn't go anywhere unless you paddle which, over the course of a day, can be pretty hard work. A real sea kayak (as opposed to the sort of open plastic bananas you can hire most places) is also a bit more complicated than a river canoe. You'll need a little instruction on how to do an 'Eskimo roll' if it tips over and how to get back in if you fall out. Sea kayak holidays, therefore, tend to involve groups, with a support boat for the longer and more challenging itineraries.

Further information

If you want to get a feel for canoeing/kayaking take a look at **www.jojaffa.com**, which is inspirational. For general information on canoeing in the UK and abroad take a look at **http://playak.com**. It's a good idea to read one of the canoeing magazines such as Canoe Focus (**www.canoefocus.demon.co.uk**).

The British Canoe Union has details of navigable rivers and courses in Britain (**www.bcu.org.uk** Tel: 0115 982 1100); Wales **www.welsh-canoeing.org.uk** Tel: 01678 521 083; Scotland **www.scot-canoe.org** Tel: 0131 317 7314; Northern Ireland **www.cani.org.uk** Tel: 0870 240 5065. For Ireland contact the Inland Waterways Association of Ireland **www.iwai.ie/rentals/rentacanoe.html** or for paddle surfing **www.kayaksurfireland.com**. For France see **www.canoe-france.com**. For links to operators everywhere try **www.responsibletravel.com** and **www.travel-quest.co.uk**.

Some specialist operators

River canoes

www.activitiesabroad.com Tel: 01670 789 991

http://adrenalinantics.com Tel: 01654 713 961

www.headwater.com Tel: 01606 720 099

www.mountainandwater.co.uk Tel: 01873 831 825

www.voyageurs.co.uk Tel: 00 353 28 2563 1730

www.pyrenean-activities.com Tel: 00 33 4 68 04 72 61 or 00 33 614 528 205

www.ardecheguides.com Tel: 00 33 4 753 70623

www.canoeoutpost.com Tel: 00 1 863 494 1215

Sea kayaks

www.seafreedomkayak.co.uk Tel: 01631 710 173

www.lakeland-horizons.co.uk Tel: 01228 521 276

www.kayakingcb.com Tel: 00 34 972 77 38 06

www.seakayak-greece.com Tel: 00 30 22840 25304

www.calkayak.com Tel: 00 1 800 366 9804

Some questions to ask

✔ Will I be on my own or part of a group?

✔ Will there be a safety boat?

✔ What happens if I get into difficulties?

✔ Will I be insured?

✔ What do I need to bring?

✔ Will there be places to buy provisions?

✔ How far each day?

✔ What is the typical age of your customers?

✔ Is this suitable for youngsters?

Who are canoe/kayak holidays for?

All sorts of people, from the adventurous to those seeking tranquillity to families with children.

Pros

● You become part of the environment and get to see scenery hidden from everyone else.

- Great for the pecs, abdos and biceps. (*Ooer! CS*)
- No noisy engine.

Cons

- Can be hard work, especially sea kayaking.
- You're rather tied to the environs of the river/beach for everything from shopping to nightlife.

Where to go

Rivers

Britain: the Dart, Dee, Isla, Severn, Spey, Thames, Usk, Wye. France: the Ardèche, Cèze, Dordogne, Drôme, Gardon, Hérault, Orb, Petit Rhône, Sorgue, Tarn, Ariège and Vezère. Spain: the Noguera Pallaresa. Portugal: the Mino, Gállego and Carasa. Florida: the Everglades National Park, the Wacissa, Aucilla and Sopchoppy Rivers.

Sea

Britain: Cornwall, Cardiff Bay, Pembrokeshire and the Scottish lochs and islands including Loch Long and the Caledonian Canal. France, Brittany and Corsica. Spain: the Costa Brava and Menorca. Italy: Sardinia. Greece: the Cyclades and Dodecanese. Florida: Key West and the Everglades. California: the Mendocino Coast.

When

Summer except for rivers like Spain's Noguera Pallaresa which only have enough water in the spring.

Price guide

A weekend in the Lake District will cost from around £200 while for a week's canoeing in France expect to pay from £750-£1,000 including ferry crossing or flight, accommodation, breakfast and evening meal. A week's sea kayak safari in Spain, sleeping on the beach, costs around £300. Accompanied day trips cost around £60. You can hire canoes/kayaks from around £40 a day.

Unusual Holiday No. 24: Sports Clinics

A holiday is a great time to learn or perfect a sport. When, otherwise, could you dedicate two entire weeks to emulating heroes such as Tiger Woods, Olga Korbut, David Beckham or Lindsay Davenport? On holiday you could put in as many hours as in two normally hectic months back home and really *achieve* something. Without the time to forget between lessons you progress faster.

The problem with sports clinics is that less dedicated or non-playing members of your family may get bored. In that case, it helps to choose a destination with plenty of other diversions on site.

Of course, you can go independently but there are often advantages to using the specialist operators. For golf, for example, green fees can be much cheaper than you'd normally pay and your operator may be able to get you onto courses that would be closed to you otherwise.

Further information

Enter the name of your chosen sport in your search engine together with the word 'holiday' or 'clinic' and your preferred destination. Specialist magazines always have holiday adverts.

If you already enjoy **golf** then a golfing holiday is an obvious thing to do. But even if you've rarely or never played this could still be for you. On a one week or two week holiday, practising and playing several hours a day, you'll advance rapidly. It's social, it's exercise without really noticing it and the ambience is generally luxurious.

For links to various specialists see **www.go-golf.net/holidays/**. Not all operators accept complete beginners – one that does (mainly Catalonia) is **www.ukschoolofgolf.com** Tel: 01702 337 020.

Some golf specialists

www.windmillhill.co.uk Tel: 0870 033 9997
www.leisurelinkgolf.com Tel: 0870 0060 7965
www.golftravelclub.com Tel: 0870 350 1107

www.serenitygolf.co.uk Tel: 0845 330 2061
www.golfbreaks.com Tel: 0800 279 7988
www.golfparexcellence.com Tel: 01737 211 818
www.golf-tours-ireland.com Tel: 00 44 28 9050 0425
www.lamangaspain.com Tel: 0800 093 2792

Tennis has a lot in common with golf – nice hotels, great locations, social life – but involves a lot more sweat. Quite often the two go together in the same clinic, which can be handy for a couple with different interests. See **www.tennisresortsonline.com** and **www.usa-tennis.de** for links to resorts and camps worldwide.

Some tennis specialists

www.lamanga-tennis.co.uk Tel: 0800 093 2792
www.brugueratennis.com Tel: 00 34 936 341 284
www.ranchovalencia.com Tel: 00 1 800 548 3664
www.holidaytennis.com Tel: 00 49 8681 9845
www.tuscanytennis.com Tel: 0141 576 7205

Have you ever wondered why some *swimmers* don't drown themselves when they have their faces in the water so long? You know, when they turn their faces sideways and open their mouths why doesn't the water all just *rush in*? Well, if you don't know the answer then a swimming clinic could do you a lot of good. Take a look at **www.swimclub.co.uk** and **www.clubswim.com/swimming-camps.asp** for links to specialist holidays, clinics and camps.

Some swimming specialists

www.holidays.swimmingwithoutstress.co.uk Tel: 01239 613 789
www.artofswimming.com/holidays.shtml Tel: 020 8446 9442
www.swimmingnature.co.uk Tel: 0870 094 9597
www.bluewatertrainingcamps.co.uk Tel: 00 38 631 832 124 or 00 33 687 287 368

Some questions to ask

✔ How many hours a day/rounds are included in the price?
✔ What clothing/equipment do I need to bring?

✓ Can I rent equipment?

✓ What standard is this clinic aimed at?

✓ Are beginners welcome?

✓ Do I need to be insured?

Who are sports holidays for?

Well, obviously, people who play golf, tennis or whatever. But also complete beginners who'd like to learn a lot in a short time.

Pros

- A whole holiday doing what you love.
- Rapid progress.

Cons

- Boring for family members who aren't as dedicated as you are.

Where to go

The possibilities are almost endless. The UK has some of the world's greatest *golf* courses, as does Ireland. For better weather Spain and Portugal are obvious choices, while, if the budget runs to it, Florida is a golfer's paradise, especially Myrtle Beach/Grand Strand, a 60 mile strip of coast with more than 100 courses. *Tennis* clinics are to be found in the same places. For *swimming* there's no need to leave the UK unless you want to.

When

If it's outdoors it has to be summer for northern Europe; any time but summer for southern Europe and Florida. If it's indoors, any time.

Price guide

Despite the upmarket image golf holidays need not be expensive. Three nights on the Algarve, two rounds and car hire cost from under £200 while seven nights on the Costa de la Luz, seven rounds and car hire cost from under £400. But, obviously, you can spend a lot more. A lot, lot more. Tennis is about the same.

And finally

The latest sport, the thing you've really got to do, is indoor climbing. Trust us. It's true. Indoor wall climbing has something 'real' climbing will never have and that's *glamour*. The craze began in America and is spreading round the world. Britain now has well over 250 walls. Indoor climbing has lots of advantages. It's far cheaper and somewhat safer than climbing mountains, it's accessible and, above all, its cool. Even sexy. To become a 'wall rat' contact the British Mountaineering Council (**www.thebmc.co.uk/indoor/walls/wall.asp** Tel: 0870 010 4878); for the world try **www.indoorclimbing.com**. Specialists include **www.keswickclimbingwall.co.uk** Tel: 017687 72000 and **www.indoorclimbing walls.co.uk** Tel: 01443 710749.

For other adventure holidays see: Chapter 1: Away From It All Holidays; Chapter 3: Holidays With Animals; Chapter 7: Extreme Holidays; Chapter 12: Snow Ball Holidays.

Chapter 5

Educational and Working Holidays

Unusual holidays in this chapter: foreign languages, painting, photography, writing, performing, archaeological digs, cookery, wine tasting, grape picking, voluntary work and much more.

The naked ape, as Desmond Morris observed, is the most curious and inventive creature that has ever lived. And the naked ape on holiday is no different. Curiosity isn't something that gets switched off that easily. On the contrary, a holiday is the perfect opportunity to learn new skills...and put them to use.

Unusual Holiday No. 25: Learn The Language

Foreign holidays and language learning go rather well together. Children, after all, learn simply by hearing, so why not adults? In fact, the adult brain loses that sponge like ability for soaking up language but combine total immersion with a degree of structure and you have the perfect method. On the basis that you learn fastest when a subject interests you, many language schools run special thematic courses – it could be food or music or hotel management or whatever. Others combine two subjects, such as Spanish with everything flamenco (**www.carmencuevas.com** Tel: 00 34 958 22 10 62). Or French with wine tasting – an excellent way of ridding students of their inhibitions (**www.is-aix.com** Tel: 00 33 4 42 93 47 90). Finally, if you stay with a local family that speaks no English you'll not only get plenty of free practice but you'll learn all those colloquial expressions the language school never mentioned.

Further information

Put 'language school' into your search engine, together with the name of the destination. At **www.abroadlanguages.com** you'll find details of and links to a wide variety of language schools.

Some specialist operators

www.cesalanguages.com Tel: 01209 211 800

www.euroacademy.co.uk Tel: 020 8297 0505

www.donquijote.org Tel: 00 34 923 277 200

www.elemadrid.com Tel: 00 34 656 851 635

www.abanico-es.com Tel: 00 34 952 20 61 82

www.accord-langues.com Tel: 00 33 1 55 33 52 33

www.scuolaleonardo.com Tel: 00 39 55 26 11 81

Who are language holidays for?

Anyone who wants to immerse themselves in not just a foreign language but also a foreign culture.

Pros

- Total immersion is the fastest way to progress, studying in the country and living with a local family.

Cons

- Expensive compared with evening classes at home or self-teaching methods such as cassettes and DVDs.

Where to go

The capital city because there are always regional accents and dialects.

When

If language is the only consideration choose the low season.

Price guide

Three hours of classes per day spread over two weeks cost around £200. Private lessons cost around £20 an hour. Language schools don't normally involve themselves in transport but can usually arrange accommodation either in shared self catering apartments or (the best) with local families. Expect to pay something like £225 for half board in a private house or £260 full board.

Unusual Holiday No. 26: Arts And Crafts

In 1890 Claude Monet, probably the best loved of all the Impressionist painters, bought some marshland next to his house in Giverny, some 50 miles outside Paris. It was there he created something that was in itself a work of environmental art, the famous water lily garden which was to be his inspiration until his death in 1926. And it can be your inspiration, too, if you take a holiday – drawing, painting or taking photographs – with ArtStudy-Giverny (**www.artstudy.com** Tel: 00 33 2 32 21 96 83).

There you will sit, actually *in Monet's garden*. Who hasn't at some time been bewitched by such a thought, the easel set up overlooking a beautiful landscape, the smell of oil paint, the floppy straw or canvas hat, and the artist ferociously appraising the scene, brush in hand? Ah, *la vie bohème*!

Try to find out as much as possible about the tutor. A brilliant artist isn't necessarily a brilliant teacher. On the other hand, it'll be all the more stimulating if your tutor produces work you admire.

Whether or not a painting holiday can actually help turn you into a Monet or a Gauguin only time will tell. It might be better not – Gauguin, after all, threw up the day job and died in poverty. But, at least while you're on holiday, you'll have a great time and be given instruction, the inspiration of convivial fellow dreamers and, most important of all, something to eat.

Of course, there's a lot more to art than painting. (In fact, anyone who follows the Turner Prize could be forgiven for thinking that art is anything but painting.) How about, for example, learning to forge some decorative ironwork? Or to make an Art Deco lampshade using the copperfoil technique devised by Louis Tiffany in the 19th century? Both courses are available at Lower Boquio Farm, Helston, Cornwall, the former given by John Christian and the latter by his wife Tricia Christian MA Glass. Or patchwork and quilting in Somerset. Or furniture restoration – bring your own furniture – on a two day course in Suffolk. Or stone carving in Wales. Or maybe furniture decoration, gilding and silver leaf based in Florence.

Further information

Just put the word 'holiday' together with your preferred medium and chosen destination into your search engine. You'll find links to art holiday specialists at **www.paintingholidaydirectory.com** and all sorts of useful information at **www.painting. about.com**.

Some specialist operators

Drawing and painting

www.headwater.com Tel: 01606 720 099 Various destinations

www.andalucian-adventures.co.uk Tel: 01453 834 137 Spain

www.artinswfrance.com Tel: 00 33 4 6876 9882 France

www.paintinginitaly.com Tel: 0800 458 9044 Italy

www.artworkshopitaly.com Tel: 00 39 347 144 5342 Italy

www.rileyarts.com Tel: 01803 722 352 Italy

www.paintgreece.com Tel: 01424 712 968 Greece

www.artexchange-greece.com Tel: 00 1 403 251 5297 Greece

www.artistacreative.com California Online booking.

Other

www.boquio.com Tel: 01209 831 694 UK Ironwork and stained glass

www.lilacbarn.co.uk Tel: 01823 690 134 UK Patchwork and quilting

Assington Mill Tel: 01787 229 955 UK Furniture restoration

www.stonecarving.co.uk Tel: 01547 528 792 Wales Stone carving

www.florenceart.net Tel: 00 39 055 714 033 Italy Furniture decoration and gilding

If you can't paint then maybe *photography* is for you. That, anyway, is how Picasso saw it. He thought photographers were frustrated artists who couldn't draw. But, then, some people think Picasso couldn't draw either. And maybe Picasso never saw Antonioni's 1966 film *Blow-up* which alerted the world to the fun David Bailey and some other photographers were having. So if you've ever fancied driving around in a convertible Roller with an aeroplane propeller sticking out of the back seat, start learning about f-numbers, depth of field and the latest digital techniques.

Further information

Put 'photographic holidays' into your search engine together with the name of the destination. For links to course providers take a look at **www.ephotozine.com/directories/listing.cfm?type=1**.

Some specialist operators

www.photoactive.co.uk Tel: 01557 331 343

www.peakphotocentre.com Tel: 01298 687 211

www.photoopportunity.co.uk Tel: 020 7388 4500

www.lightandland.co.uk Tel: 01432 839 111

www.lakelandphotohols.com Tel: 01768 778 459

www.wildshots.co.uk Tel: 01540 651 352

www.skyeinfocus.co.uk 01471 822 264

www.Tirnameala.com Tel: 00 353 26 45651

www.learninitaly.com Tel: 041 535 1140

Our home, an ancient water mill, was built mostly of stones and earth quite a long time ago. When we came along we decided to slap a bit of mortar on it for good measure. But it had stood up for a few hundred years without it. There's something truly magical, even mystical, about *dry stone walling*. It appeals to people who would never dream of tackling brickwork (which is far easier). It's an art, yes, but it's also extremely physical. So any course on dry stone walling is going to be something of a working holiday. You're going to be building somebody's wall, not just stacking heavy stones for the fun of it. So if you're at all particular who benefits from your labour choose accordingly. If you're not particular, drop in here any time – there's plenty more restoration still to do.

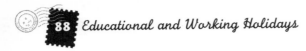

Further information

Put 'dry stone wall holiday' into your search engine together with the name of the destination.

Some specialist operators

www.shantigriha.com Tel: 01854 633 260
www.drystone-walling.co.uk Tel: 01539 441 985
www.drystone-walls.com Tel: 01668 219 818
www.tamarackbushcraft.co.uk Tel: 01995 670 101

Everybody can write. Right? So what is there to learn on a *writing* holiday? Well, first of all there are all those unusual disciplines that have their own very special needs – film scripts, radio plays, press releases and so on. But the most vital thing is marketing. Why? Because the pool of writers is expanding even faster than the growth of new media. Never has writing been such a competitive job – nor, for the most part, so poorly rewarded. (*I'm playing the violin. Ed.*)

Whether it's for personal satisfaction or professional, a writing course can put you ahead. And it's certainly not a case of those that can, do, those that can't, teach, because some extremely well known and successful writers are getting involved.

Further information

Put 'writing holidays' into your search engine together with the name of the destination. For links to writing holidays see **www.author-network.com/courses.html**.

Some specialist operators

www.newforest-online.co.uk/writeforest Tel: 01590 624 098 UK
www.highgreen-arts.co.uk Tel: 0207 602 1363 UK
www.emerson.org.uk Tel: 01342 822 238 UK
www.author-network.com/blumenthal.html Tel: 07786 057 904 UK
www.roselle-angwin.co.uk Tel: 01822 841 081 UK
www.hfholidays.co.uk Tel: 020 8905 9556 UK

www.writehereinfrance.co.uk Tel: 00 33 5 65 997645 France
www.hotelfinca.com Tel: 00 34 952 030 444 Spain
www.worldspirit.org.uk Online booking Greece
www.skyros.co.uk Tel: 020 7267 4424 Greece
www.writeonholiday.co.uk Tel: 01422 845 819 Turkey

If you have absolutely no artistic talent of any sort whatsoever, well, you can still at least learn to *appreciate* art. So how about joining *Antiques Roadshow* expert Marc Allum and his wife Lisa Lloyd at their home Château Coÿe, Pau, France? As you'd expect, it's decorated with an impressive collection of furniture, art and antiques. A five day course, Monday to Friday, might include half a dozen lectures and talks, visits to historical sites in the area and insight into a few tricks of the trade (**www.chateaucoye.com** Tel: 00 33 5 58 797 209).

Some questions to ask

✔ What qualifications do your tutors have?
✔ What basic skills do I need?
✔ Will this course help me professionally or is it purely for hobbyists?
✔ Will the course include help with marketing my work?
✔ What is the tutor/student ratio?
✔ What media does the course cover?
✔ Do I need to bring materials/equipment?
✔ Will I be able to buy materials locally?
✔ How many others will be on the course?
✔ Is teaching done in a formal or informal way?
✔ How many hours of tuition will I receive each day?
✔ What other things are there to do in the area?

Who are arts and crafts holidays for?

People who want to improve their skills for professional reasons or just as a hobby.

Pros

● Instruction in the company of fellow enthusiasts.
● Useful networking contacts.

Cons

● Lots of distractions (beaches, restaurants etc).

Where to go

Holiday courses are usually in areas of outstanding natural beauty. If you find inspiration elsewhere you may have difficulty finding a suitable course.

When

Any time.

Price guide

Holiday courses in painting, crafts, photography and writing tend to cost from around £350 including lunch but no accommodation and from £500 a week half board, whether in the UK or abroad, excluding travel. But they can go up to as much as £1,000. The two day furniture restoration course at Assington Mill, Suffolk costs just over £100, including lunch. The three day courses in forged iron or stained glass at Boquio Farm cost around £225 including lunch – or for £300 you can have undivided attention. Five days at Chateau Coÿe costs £800, not including flights.

Unusual Holiday No. 27: Music, Theatre And Dance

It's nearly 30 years ago now that Gillian and David Johnston started Harpenden Musicale in the front room of their home. From that tiny beginning has come a successful community music school and the highly acclaimed Musicale Holiday, offering children summer music tuition all over the country (**www.musicale.co.uk** Tel: 01582 460 978). There are two kinds of courses, those for instrumentalists up to the age of 16 and those for children five to nine who don't yet play an instrument.

Between us we've had a go at the piano, violin, guitar, cello and clarinet. And more or less given them all up. So we need the inspiration of a summer school, too. And, fortunately, an organisation known as Contemporary Music Making for Amateurs is just the job. COMA runs an award winning summer school which is not so much for child prodigies as for adults like us looking for something friendly and non-competitive. (So can we bring our kazoo?) The 'taster' sessions are a great opportunity to have a go at new things and it doesn't all stop until the last notes of the nightly jam sessions (**www.coma.org** Tel: 020 7247 7736).

If you've ever broken into *O sole mio* in the shower or while eating an ice cream then a holiday in Salerno, Italy with Musykando is just for you (**www.musykando.com** Tel: 020 7394 4326). Under the guidance of an expert in Neapolitan music you'll perform with local singers while, no doubt, a *paloma blanca* or two flutter overhead. If a solo role is more your ambition then the versatile Sally Bradshaw is your coach (**www.songful.net**). Sally has sung everything from duets with Sting to Handel's Agrippina and teaches all over the world, including at Shanti Griha, Dundonnell, Scotland (**www.shantigriha.com** Tel: 01854 633 260). If you'd like to understand more about opera without actually singing yourself try Operaphile (**www.dantealighieri. com** Tel: 00 39 0577 49533). You'll spend two hours a day studying opera (in English), two hours a day studying Italian, learn about Italian culture, do some Italian cooking and visit the opera at Verona, Torre del Lago or Florence.

*

Imagine attending a New York Film Academy acting summer camp at Universal Studios, Hollywood. Perhaps Johnny Depp or Sharon Stone will come strolling by. Who knows? For sure you'll spend a week you'll probably never forget. And you might even end up famous. If you can't afford to get to California (and what aspiring actor can?) the Academy also runs courses in Oxford (**www.nyfa.com/summercamps/index.html** Tel: 01865 271 805). Or you could follow the home grown route that gave us such actors as Diana Rigg and Ralph Fiennes by taking a short course at RADA (**www.radaenterprises.org** Tel: 020 7908 4747). They say humour is the hardest thing of all so a few tips from stand-up comedian and Edinburgh Fringe Finalist Zero Gibson might come in handy. Held in Roujan, France, Zero's courses last three days (**www.7 daywonder. com** Tel: 0871 734 1165). After all that, you'll be ready to audition. Exactly how is the subject of a one-week course in Chiswick (**www.artsed.co.uk** Tel: 020 8987 66 44).

*

In 1915 the tango was a craze and now it's back again. There are *milongas* (gatherings) everywhere, including the Dome in London, Le Chantier Ephémère in Paris and Triangular Studio, New York (**www.tangonyc.com** Tel: 00 1 212 633 6445). But probably the best place short of Buenos Aires is Miami. Club Dance Holidays (**www.danceholidays.com** Tel: 0870 286 6000) will take you there for the annual Tango Festival where you can dance all night. If you don't know how to do it then you can sign up for a course. Our encyclopaedia says it's 'fast, sensual and disreputable'. (*Count me in. PJ*)

Further information

Put 'summer school' or 'master class' into your search engine together with your chosen subject and the name of your destination. You can see a list of music summer schools at **www.summer-schools.info**. Details of international competitions are available from the World Federation of International Music Competitions (**www.wfimc.org** Tel: 00 42 23 21 36 20).

Some specialist operators

Music
www.dartingtonsummerschool.org.uk Tel: 01803 847 077
www.uppinghamsummerschool.co.uk Tel: 01572 820 800
http://dorsetopera.com Tel: 01258 840 000
www.musiceverything.com Tel: 020 8241 2277
www.lmfl.com/orchestra.htm Tel: 01454 419 504
www.impulse-music.co.uk Tel: 0118 950 7865
www.suzukimusic.net Tel: 01372 720 088
www.quecumbar.co.uk Tel: 020 7787 2227
www.austrian-master-classes.com Tel: 00 43 662 870 844
www.marimbacompetition.com Tel: 00 32 11 34 87 35

Dance
www.hfholidays.co.uk Tel: 020 8905 9556
www.bellydancingholidays.co.uk Tel: 07956 286 166
www.vivaflamencopromotions.com Tel: 0870 011 3347
www.partyweekender.com Tel: 020 8593 1947

Some questions to ask
✔ What level do I need to be?
✔ Will we be putting on any kind of show at the end?
✔ What qualifications does the tutor have?

Who are theatre, music and dance holidays for?
It helps to have a little talent but enthusiasm counts for a lot.

Pros
● Get together with fellow enthusiasts and performers.

Cons
● You could be intimidated if the level is too high.

Where to go
Anywhere that's good.

When
Any time.

Price guide
Five day Musicale Holiday courses cost around £160 (tuition and musical activities only). COMA's summer school costs around £400 for five nights full board. Operaphile costs from around £750 for two weeks. A week's summer camp in Hollywood costs around £700 while two weeks at RADA will be £1,000 (tuition only). Zero's three day courses in making people laugh cost £250 including accommodation and food but not flights. A week's course in audition technique is around £220. Dance weekends in the UK can cost from around £100; think in terms of £500 for a week in Turkey including flight, half board and 10 hours of tuition, or for a week in Granada learning flamenco.

Unusual Holiday No. 28: Time Travel

When did human beings appear on the Earth? It's a rather intriguing question. What would you say? One hundred thousand years ago? Two hundred thousand? Well, if you're talking *Homo sapiens*, our own species, then the oldest known remains date from 160,000 years ago. But if you're talking *hominids*, the term now used for all members of the human family, then we're talking – wait for it – six to seven *million* years ago. When you get involved in archaeology that's the kind of time travel you're capable of. In fact, as a holiday volunteer, you probably won't get your hands on anything quite so old (or valuable) but you certainly could play your part in excavating remains 1.7 *million* years old. That's the age attributed by palaeontologists to human made tools found at Orce, Andalucia. Tools that you, too, could be unearthing (**www.responsibletravel.com** – online only). Through the same company you could also join a dig at Deia, Mallorca, at a site once inhabited by the Bell Beaker culture. You'll perhaps spend your mornings digging, your afternoons washing, sorting and classifying finds and your evenings discussing the significance of the day's discoveries.

If you'd rather just admire the work that other archaeologists have already done then tour operators such as Swan Hellenic, Explore and Andante could be for you (contact details below). For a one day introduction to archaeology in the Peak District in the company of Dr Ian Heath see **www.pdat.co.uk** (Tel: 0778 253 3271).

Further information

For information about what's going on in the world of archaeology contact the European Association of Archaeologists **www.e-a-a.org** (Tel: 00 420 257 014 411) or put 'history holiday' into your search engine together with the name of your chosen destination.

Some specialist operators

www.gruppiarcheologici.org Online only – two week camps all over Italy

www.earthwatch.org/Europe Tel: 01865 318 838

www.explore.co.uk Tel: 0870 333 4001
www.andantetravels.co.uk Tel: 01722 713 800
www.swanhellenic.com Tel: 0845 355 5111

Some questions to ask

✔ What kind of work will I be doing?
✔ How many hours work per day?
✔ What is the standard of accommodation?
✔ Does the price include all meals?

Who are time travel holidays for?

Digs are hard and sometimes tedious work so you need to be pretty dedicated.

Pros

● You'll learn a lot and participate in the excitement of discovery.

Cons

● You pay quite a lot for the privilege of hard work and basic accommodation.

Where to go

Archaeological sites are everywhere.

When

Summer – rain isn't beneficial.

Price guide

One-day tours in the Peak District cost around £50 for adults and £35 for children. Andante will take you on a seven night tour of eastern Ireland's rich archaeological heritage for £1,400 fully inclusive. Working holidays to Orce and Deia cost from just over £1,000 up to around £1,200 for 14 days. For that you'll get basic accommodation and meals but not flights.

Unusual Holiday No. 29: Food, Wine And Grape Picking

Some people, as the saying goes, eat to live while others live to eat. Same thing for holidays. Some people go to eat on holiday while others go on holiday to eat. (And drink.) If you're in the latter category why not, as it were, go the whole hog and book a cookery course?

We've all come a long way since Fanny and Johnny Craddock and toad in the hole. We're all foodies now and we've all got the recipe books to prove it but there's nothing like a practical demonstration.

Find out as much as you can about the chef. See if he or she has written a book, like Rosemary Barron, who leads a Tasting Places holiday on the Greek island of Santorini and who wrote *Flavours of Greece*. Check out the recipes to see if they're the kind of thing you want to do.

It's not, by any means, all hell – or even heaven – in the kitchen. Most holidays include visits to local markets, vineyards, producers of local specialities and, of course, restaurants.

Further information

Some specialist operators

Various destinations
www.tastingplaces.com Tel: 020 8964 5333
www.headwater.com Tel: 01606 720 099
www.holidayonthemenu.com Tel: 0870 8 99 88 44
www.creativitytravel.com Tel: 01227 276 390

France
www.cookinfrance.com Tel: 00 33 5 53 302 405
www.realfoodfrance.co.uk Online booking
www.villavalentina.com Online booking

Italy
www.atg-oxford.co.uk Tel: 01865 315 678

www.italiansecrets.co.uk Tel: 020 8871 4888

www.vinaio.com Tel: 00 39 055 234 6511

Greece

www.laskarina.co.uk Tel: 01444 880 385

www.cuisineinternational.com Tel: 00 1 214 3731 161

Where we live (in Alt Empordá, Spain) people pool their grapes at the local *cooperativa*. In fact, there are about 10 we can visit within a 30 minute drive. Every year we tour around them to decide which wine is best this time. Not that we know anything much about wine, you understand. We just know what we like. (And, after all, most of it costs less than £1 a litre.) It's, what shall we say, an *unpretentious* little way of making a wine tour. Which you can do not only here but in every other wine-producing region of Spain.

There are far grander, of course, with much swirling and gargling and 'hint of tobacco' and all the rest of it. A good place to get started, without even leaving the UK, is Berry Bros & Rudd which runs wine tastings and wine dinners in its vaulted cellars in St. James's Street, London, as well as locations around the country. If you want to do something a little more structured the London Wine Academy runs classes one night a week for six weeks. There are courses for complete beginners as well as those wanting to improve their knowledge of Bordeaux, Burgundy, Champagne and so on.

Armed with your newly acquired knowledge you can sally forth among the *chateaux*, confident that you'll never again make a *faux pas*. Such as saying how much you prefer claret to Bordeaux. So why not motor over to the Loire or Burgundy with Grape Escapes? There is a problem with self-drive wine holidays, though. The driver can't actually, ahem, *taste* very much of the stuff. La Grande Maison d'Arthenay solves that by chauffeuring you around the Saumur vineyards so you can assess as much as you like. Probably the ultimate in hedonism are the tours run by Alabaster and Clarke (see winetours below). Their Ultimate Champagne, for example, will take you to the cellars and sometimes the dining tables of such august and famous establishments as Bollinger, Pol

Roger, Louis Roederer and Moët & Chandon, with accommodation to match.

There is another way of learning about wine. And instead of *you* paying *them*, *they* pay *you*. Now that's more like it! It's called grape picking. Ideal for a two week holiday. The only drawback is that it's hard work. Very hard work. We know. We've done it. We can report that nature's biggest design error is the human back. It just cannot cope. Learning about wine is not the primary aim, of course, but during your work and over lunch and the evening meal you'll probably pick up far more practical knowledge than on most courses. You'll vastly improve your language skills. You'll have accommodation. And you'll get paid, well, not a fortune but at least the legal minimum for the country concerned.

Further information

Some specialist operators

Wine holidays and courses
www.bbr.com Tel: 0870 900 4300
www.londonwineacademy.com Tel: 0870 100 0 100/020 7553 9754
www.winetours.co.uk Tel: 01730 893 344
www.lagrandemaison.net Tel: 00 33 2 41 40 35 06
www.grapeescapes.net Tel: 08707 667 617
www.activitiesabroad.com/wine/ Tel: 01670 789 991

Grape picking
www.pickingjobs.com
www.apcon.nl Tel: 00 31 505 492 435

Some questions to ask

Cookery
✓ How many hours a day in the kitchen?
✓ Domestic or professional equipment?
✓ What style of cuisine?
✓ How many others will be on the course?
✓ Will we be visiting local markets, producers and restaurants?

Wine

✔ How many wineries will we visit each day?

✔ Will we be offered facilities not available to the general public?

Grape picking

✔ How many hours a day?

✔ Is the land flat or terraced?

✔ Are the grapes close to the ground or on wires?

✔ Will I be paid by the hour or by quantity?

✔ What accommodation is provided?

✔ What meals are provided?

Who are food, wine and grape picking holidays for?

Grape picking is only for the young and fit but cooking, eating and wine tasting are for anybody with enthusiasm.

Pros

● Gourmandism isn't part of the holiday, it *is* the holiday.

Cons

● Grape picking is only fun with the right people because it's very hard work. On the other hand, 'foodie' holidays tend to be a little sedentary.

Where to go

France is the big destination for everything to do with food and wine but Spain, Italy, Greece and even the UK are pretty good, too.

When

Grape picking normally takes place in September. Cooking, eating and drinking any time.

Price guide

Berry Bros & Rudd wine tastings and wine dinners cost from around £35 up to almost £100, depending on the food and wine. London Wine Academy courses cost approaching £250. Self-drive holidays to the Continent's vineyards cost from around £350 a week up to £1,000.

Alabaster and Clarke's four nights Ultimate Champagne costs just under £2,000 as does their seven night holiday to California's Napa Valley.

Unusual Holiday No. 30: Educating Rita...And Richard

Ever feel embarrassed that you didn't have a 'proper' education? Didn't go to Oxford or Cambridge? Well, that's fairly easily put right with a small amount of time and a fairly large amount of money. (There's always a snag, isn't there?) Both institutions run summer schools (**www.cont-ed.cam.ac.uk** Tel: 01954 280 280 and **www.oasp.ac.uk** Tel:01865 793 333) where prices range from a few hundred pounds up to several thousand when accommodation is included.

In fact, all over the UK and Europe every summer there are universities fighting, yes fighting, for your attendance with barely a mention of previous qualifications. (Funny how they're so important in the winter but not the summer.) And the variety of subjects is staggering. Want to study the impact of European enlargement, so you can hold forth in the pub come autumn? Then set off for Cervia, Italy (**www.unibo.it**) or Limerick, Ireland (**www.ul.ie** Tel: 353 61 20 22 02). Want to be an expert on European Union Law? Then it's off to Brussels (**www.ulb.ac.be**). Shakespeare, medieval Britain, geometric modelling, the life cycle of the aphid...the list is endless.

But it's not only late starting adults who can benefit from a summer holiday at university. Children can, too. Strathclyde University, for example, takes 250 schoolchildren a fortnight for what it calls 'stealth learning' (**www.strath.ac.uk/summer academy** Tel: 0141 950 3542). Children are said to go back to school with greater motivation and higher aspirations. The Sutton Trust runs summer schools at Oxford, Cambridge, Bristol and Nottingham for Year 12 state school pupils with non-professional parents (**www.suttontrust.com** Tel: 020 8788 3223). The students choose one subject and attend lectures and tutorials just like undergraduates. They can also take part in the extra-curricular activities which might include rowing or ice-skating or other things they haven't tried before. Through it all they're guided by an undergraduate mentor. And here's the really good bit. The week on campus is *free*.

Further information

For details of all kinds of courses see **www.summer-schools.info**.

Some questions to ask

✔ Is the accommodation on campus?
✔ Will I have a private room?
✔ Will I have to share bathroom facilities?
✔ Is there any kind of exam or diploma at the end?
✔ Will other university facilities be available, such as sports?

Who are university holidays for?

Mostly those who missed out before.

Pros

● Tuition of a very high standard.

Cons

● You don't get any letters after your name.

Where to go

Universities everywhere.

When

Summer.

Price guide

Think in terms of £300-£400 a week including accommodation and food (but not transport).

Unusual Holiday No. 31:
Make The World A Better Place

Can you as an individual make a constructive difference to the world? In the face of so much destruction it often seem hopeless. And yet the evidence is right there. Take Trees for Life, for example. Since 1989 this charity, mostly with the help of volunteers, has planted 429,500 native trees in the Caledonian Forest. Today the forest covers less than one per cent of its former range in the Highlands of Scotland but the charity aims to restore it to 600 square miles. And it will. Once again it will become an important habitat for threatened species such as the wild cat, pine marten, red squirrel, Scottish crossbill, capercaillie and black grouse as well as others to be reintroduced.

All very noble. But how can you both work and have a holiday at the same time? In fact, it's not just a one way process. Yes, you give your time and labour but as a volunteer you'll be privileged to go places and experience things that are denied to ordinary tourists.

The restoration of the Caledonian Forest is just one example of individuals making the world a better place. There are many others. The National Trust, for example, runs some 450 different working holiday projects each year in its efforts to maintain the 30,000 properties for which it is responsible. Other charities are involved in everything from cleaning beaches to promoting environmental awareness in schools.

Further information

Be clear at the outset how much work you're prepared to do, what living conditions you're willing to accept and how much free time you need. The better run projects allow plenty of time off for leisure activities in the surrounding area.

Earth Restoration Service (**www.earthrestorationservice.org** Tel: 00 33 4 68 26 41 79) is an umbrella organisation with links to worthwhile projects all over the world. If you're just looking for a working holiday try **www.payaway.co.uk**.

Some specialist operators

www.nationaltrust.org.uk/volunteers Tel: 0870 609 5383
www.earthwatch.org/Europe Tel: 01865 318 838
www.worldwideexperience.com Tel: 01483 860 560
www.treesforlife.org.uk Tel: 01309 691 292
www.sunseed.org.uk Tel: 00 34 950 525 770
www.rempart.com Tel: 00 33 1 4271 9655

Who are make-the-world-better holidays for?

Everybody should do it sometime.

Pros

- The feel-good factor.
- You may experience things denied to ordinary tourists and go places they can't go.
- You may acquire useful skills.

Cons

- You have to pay to work hard in often difficult conditions.

Where to go

The world needs sorting out just about everywhere.

When

Usually the summer.

Price guide

Although you'll be working a lot of the time you'll nevertheless have to pay something for your holiday. In many cases, this could be well under £100 to include basic accommodation and meals (often vegetarian). National Trust working holidays, for example, start at about £60 a week. The cost of getting there will be on top. Some working holidays, on the other hand, are incredibly expensive. That doesn't make them a rip off if your money is going to charity or to do good things, but if the price seems unreasonable to you it's certainly worth asking for a breakdown of where it all goes. We're a little bit sceptical about some companies whose working holidays, in uncomfortable conditions, cost far more than 'proper' holidays in luxurious hotels.

And finally

Have you got a 'dream' job? Something you've always fantasised about? To be a choreographer? A stylist working for TV or the movies? A theatre producer? A golf pro? Well, an organisation called VocationVacations can organise it for you (**www.vocationsvacations.com** Tel: 01273 206 152). It's a bit like the story of Cinderella because although the dream may not end at midnight on the first day it's certainly all over by midnight on the second – and back you go to washing the floor. And two very expensive days at that. Typically you'll be paying £500 or more, depending on the dream. But hang on! Let's think about this. *You* pay *them* for *letting* you do it. Huh? *(Message to our publishers: don't go getting any ideas.)*

Other educational and working holidays: Chapter 1: Castaway Holidays; Chapter 3: Holidays With Animals.

Chapter 6

Mind, Body and Spirit Holidays

Unusual holidays in this chapter: yoga, pilates, meditation, reiki, spas, pilgrimages and much more.

There comes a time when a holiday just isn't, well, *holiday* enough. When lying on the beach just isn't rest enough. You need something extra to revitalise the body, still the mind and let the spirit soar.

Unusual Holiday No. 32: Alternative Holidays

We're pretty cynical people (journalists normally are) but we've tried quite a few things over the years out of curiosity – tai chi, yoga, pilates, reiki, massage, meditation, aromatherapy, homeopathy, hypnotherapy, naturopathy and more. Some produced benefits, some did nothing at all and one or two were downright harmful. Our opinion (for what it's worth) is that 'alternatives' shouldn't generally be regarded as therapies at all – that's to say, as treatments for specific illnesses – but simply as ways of enhancing your pleasure in life. Yoga and pilates undeniably improve agility and strength, aromas, colours and music clearly affect mood, and proper nutrition is obviously essential to health. But don't go looking for miracle cures on your alternative holiday. Just go looking for new experiences, interesting friends and a nice time. And, if you're lucky, perhaps you'll come back a little changed and with a new way of looking at the world.

If you're a bit confused by the ever growing catalogue of alternatives, here's a quick rundown of some of the more widely available techniques together with the claims (we stress *claims*) made for them:

Acupuncture: The insertion of fine needles into the body's channels of energy (Qi) to balance Yin and Yang and stimulate the body's own healing response.

Alexander Technique: A way of sitting, standing, breathing and moving that reduces pressure and enhances movement.

Aromatherapy: The use of plant oils to help the body balance and heal itself.

Ayurveda: A Sanskrit word meaning 'science of longevity' – food and lifestyle for self-healing.

Bowen Therapy: Small, gentle movements at specific points on the body for the treatment of sports injuries and other problems.

Chiropractic: The treatment of spinal problems married to a philosophy of natural health.

Flower Essences: Similar to homeopathy, using flower remedies to promote healing.

Herbal Medicine: Using herbs for medicinal purposes.

Holistic Counselling: Using a range of techniques to increase intuition and release the real self.

Homeopathy: Curing through minute doses of plant, animal or mineral substances that create the same symptoms as the illness being treated.

Hypnotherapy: The implanting of new beliefs at the subconscious level while the patient is in a trance.

Intuitive Art: Putting the emphasis on the artistic process rather than the outcome.

Kinesiology: Muscle monitoring to identify imbalances.

Life coaching: An expert gives long term advice.

Macrobiotics: Diet based on the principle of Yin and Yang, utilising lots of brown rice and very severe at its ultimate level.

Massage: Manipulation of the whole body to relieve aches and pains and promote relaxation.

Meditation: Embracing a whole range of techniques for quietening the mind and experiencing a sense of peace.

Naturopathy: Assisting the body's own natural healing abilities through proper nutrition, herbal medicine and exercise.

Neuroskeletal Dynamics (NSD): Light pressure to stimulate the nervous system.

Pilates: Exercises to tone and lengthen muscles without impacting the joints.

Reflexology: Manipulating reflex points on the feet (and sometimes hands) in the belief that each one is related to a specific part of the body.

Reiki: Placing hands close to the body to transfer energy and promote healing.

Shiatsu: Massage and the use of pressure, rather than needles, on the acupuncture points to release toxins and stimulate the immune system.

Yoga: Exercises for agility and strength combined with philosophy to join individual consciousness with Universal Consciousness.

WARNING
For many 'alternatives' there are no legally recognised practices or qualifications. Standards may vary considerably. Scientists dispute many of the claims made. For a cold scientific analysis take a look at www.quackwatch.org.

So what do they do for you, these alternative holidays? What happens? Well, obviously, every place is different. But yoga is pretty much a mainstay, nowadays. So your day will probably start with a series of *asanas* or postures as well as exercises in *pranayama*, or breathing technique. And perhaps finish with meditation. Or it might just as easily finish with a nightcap at the bar – alternative doesn't have to mean strict. Yoga might be nothing more than a form of exercise – or you might get into the philosophical aspect, that the whole purpose is to reunite the self (jiva) with the pure consciousness (Brahman). Then there may be a range of other activities on offer such as dancing, aerobics, pilates, tai chi, singing, painting, hiking, riding and swimming.

We'd recommend you to stick with the things like that, that are proven to be healthy or at least harmless and avoid anything dubious, potentially dangerous or downright expensive.

Some alternative holidays are more alternative than others. If you're looking for something 'way out' try camping in the Santa Cruz Mountains of California for the Firedance Festival, which for five days in August is a celebration of drum, dance and song (**www.firedance.org** Tel: 00 1 866 436 4420). No doubt you'll get to hug a few trees as well.

Further information

You can get a few ideas by visiting the Mind, Body, Spirit Festival at London's Royal Horticultural Halls, usually around the end of May. There's also a Wellbeing Show at the same venue in November as well as a Northern Festival at the G-Mex, Manchester, around the end of September/early October. (Information on all three is at **www.mindbodyspirit.co.uk** Tel: 020 7371 9191.) Another source of inspiration is the One World Summer Festival held in Hampshire in August for six days and featuring over 200 workshops in physical and spiritual development (**www.macrobios.com** Tel: 01273 249 770).

For general information and links try **www.places-to-be.com**, **www.retreatsonline.com** and **www.ninedeadlyvenoms.com/travel.htm**.

Some specialist operators

www.therapies.com Tel: 01256 881 050 UK
www.heartspring.co.uk Tel: 01267 241 999 UK
www.holyisland.org Tel: 01770 601 100 UK
www.lindisfarne.org.uk Tel: 01289 389 222. UK.
www.earthseaspirit.com Tel: 0870 766 8252 France
www.beyondretreats.co.uk Tel: 020 7226 4044 France
www.yogafrance.com Tel: 00 33 5 65 364 351 France
www.asuraspain.com Tel: 00 34 958 851 513 Spain
www.spanish-reflections.co.uk Online booking Spain
www.spanishspiritholidays.com Online booking Spain
www.mallorcaspirit.com Online booking Spain
www.sunflowerretreats.com Tel: 0116 259 9422 Italy
www.skyros.co.uk Tel: 0207 267 4424 Greece
www.newagehealthspa.com Tel: 00 1 845 985 7600 New York State

Some questions to ask

✔ What qualifications do your therapists/instructors have?
✔ How long have they been practising?
✔ What proof is there of the benefits claimed for this?
✔ Will I be expected to take part in certain activities or can I do what I want?
✔ Are all courses included or are some extra?
✔ Are children allowed?
✔ What other things are there to do in the area?

Who are 'alternative' holidays for?

Interest is a sure sign of middle age.

Pros

● You may return a better person.

Cons

● Then, again, you may not. Watch out for (a) 'gurus' who are at best incompetent and at worst charlatans; (b) 'spiritual' as a euphemism applied to accommodation and meaning 'tacky'.

Where to go

The UK, France, Spain, Italy, Greece and California.

When

Summer – but the Mediterranean, Florida and California can also be great escapes from the British winter.

Price guide

Most operators don't get involved in travel arrangements so you'll probably have to book your own flights where necessary. You can cut costs by choosing a retreat served by a no-frills airline. Typically a week will cost around £500 half board including the course. The New Age Health Spa in New York State costs from around £115 a night per person.

Unusual Holiday No. 33: Spas

Whereas for 'alternative' holidays a remote and beautiful location is virtually essential, that isn't the case with spas. A nice view is always pleasant but a spa break can as easily be in the centre of London or Manchester as a remote island. Spa treatments tend to take place indoors. Okay, outside there may be a running track, a tennis court or a garden but, let's be honest, we're really talking beauty treatments interspersed with periods of total immobility. Men can go, of course, and do, but even in the USA, they're only 29% of spa customers. So this is much more something for the ladies.

The Sanctuary, in London's Covent Garden, for example, encourages women to amble around naked and won't even let men in. (*Shame. PJ*) It's all white towelling robes, candles, massages and facials although, admittedly, there are plunge and exercise pools.

A massage is the one thing that almost all spa visitors indulge in so the masseur's skill is fundamental. You should know within a few minutes whether or not you feel good about him or her. One way to judge is the variety of techniques used to pummel you. Fingers, thumbs and palms certainly. Score extra for knuckles, fists and even elbows. You should end up with your muscles soothed, your blood circulation improved and your anxieties dispelled.

Having said that spas are mostly for women there are a few exclusively for men (like Nickel Spa in New York) and there's a move to encourage couples. That makes it much more of a holiday. Think of hot tubs for two and side-by-side massage tables in front of an open fire. In America they excel at this. Try the Spa at New York's Mandarin Oriental, overlooking Central Park; the Mirbeau in upstate Skaneateles with its claw foot baths and Monet-inspired gardens; or the Calistoga Ranch in Upper Napa Valley, California, set in private gardens of 157 acres.

Further information

Take a look at **www.spabreak.co.uk** (Tel: 01883 724 843) an agency specialising in spas, or put 'spa' into your search engine together with the name of the destination. For a specialist operator see **www.bodyandsoulholidays.com** (Tel: 020 7594 0290). For general information, especially on the USA, see **http://spas. about.com**.

Some spas

www.thesanctuary.co.uk Tel: 0870 770 3350 UK

www.thegrove.co.uk Tel: 01923 807 807 UK

www.wellbeingnow.co.uk Tel: 01628 670 970 UK

www.champneys.com Tel: 08703 300 300 UK

www.parkkenmare.com Tel: 00 353 644 1200 Ireland

www.sources-caudalie.com Tel: 00 33 5 57 83 83 83 France

www.hotelbotanico.com Tel: 00 34 922 381 400 Tenerife

www.ilsanpietro.it Tel: 00 39 0898 25455 Italy

www.villadeste.it Tel: 00 39 0313 481 Italy

www.victoria-jungfrau.ch Tel: 00 41 338 28 28 28 Switzerland

www.aldemarhotels.com Tel: 00 30 210 623 6150 Crete

www.thanohotels.com Tel: 357 268 88 000 Cyprus

www.calistogaranch.com Tel: 00 1 707 254 2800 California

www.mandarinoriental.com Tel: 00 1 212 866 801 8880 New York

www.cornelia.com Tel: 00 1 212 871 3050 New York

www.blissworld.com Tel: 00 1 212 219 8970 New York

www.silkdayspa.com Tel: 00 1 212 255 6457 New York

www.mirbeau.com Tel: 00 1 315 685 1927 Skaneateles. New York State

Some questions to ask

✓ Where has the therapist studied?

✓ How many hours of training has he/she had?

✓ What beauty treatments are available?

✓ What treatments (facials, massages etc) are included in the price?

✓ Do I have to be naked for a massage?

✓ Do you have facilities for couples?

Who are spa holidays for?

Anyone who wants to be pampered and (usually) passive.

Pros

● A healthy glow without too much exertion.

Cons

● Not generally suitable for children or those who crave vigorous activity.

Where to go

For treatment there's really no need to leave the UK but for a spa *holiday* it's hard to beat America.

When

Any time.

Price guide

A day at the Sanctuary, London, costs around £80. For one night at a UK spa think in terms of £100 including accommodation, dinner, breakfast and access to all facilities. Look for fully inclusive deals that include facials (normally from around £35 up to around £100) and massages. A weekend at a spa in France, including flights and two nights on a b&b basis will cost from around £400. A room at the Mandarin Oriental, New York, costs from around £300 a night while an 80 minute facial in the Spa costs around £160.

Unusual Holiday No. 34: The Pilgrimage To Santiago de Compostela

There are plenty of holy sites in Europe but one stands out as a site of pilgrimage. That's to say, the journey itself is the important thing. It is the medieval route to Santiago de Compostela in northern Spain, said to be the burial place of St James, brother of John the Evangelist and one of the 12 apostles. Pilgrimages there began in the 10th century. There were four main routes across France all entering Spain at Roncesvalles. One begins at Paris, one at Vézelay, one at Le Puy and one at Arles. Beginning at Seville there is also the Ruta de la Plata (Silver Way) which heads north for 690 km before joining the way from Roncesvalles at Astorga – with another 10 days still to go. But, generally, it's the route from Le Puy that's considered the most attractive at 1,400 km/875 miles. This was the route first taken by Godescalc, Bishop of le Puy in 950 AD. From Roncesvalles all follow the same line through Pamplona, Logroño, Burgos, Léon and Sarria to Santiago. It's the chunk known as the Camino Francés and the section on which you're most likely to meet other pilgrims and make friends. You'll know them by the scallop shell symbols on their backpacks or hats – it's been the emblem since the 12th century and is also used to mark the route.

If you want to be able to prove you've made the pilgrimage you'll need the *Credencial del Peregrino* (Pilgrim's Credential) which you can get at Roncesvalles or a *refugio* in other major cities along the route. You must then get it stamped once a day at the *refugios* you pass. In order to qualify for the Compostela certificate (obtained from The Pilgrims Office in Santiago) you must walk the final 100 km/62 miles. In fact, the only 'real' ways of making the pilgrimage are on foot, by bicycle or on horseback – making it an exercise for mind, body and spirit simultaneously.

Further information

Several travel companies can organise your pilgrimage on part or all of the route, transporting your luggage each day. Take a look at

www.worldwalks.com (Tel: 01242 254 353) and, for the last week of the route only, **www.exodus.co.uk** (Tel: 0870 240 5550). Cyclists should contact **www.discoverytravel.co.uk** (Tel: 01904 766 564).

Some questions to ask

✔ Will I qualify for a Compostela certificate?

✔ Is it necessary to be a believer?

✔ How far will we be walking/cycling/riding each day?

✔ What style of accommodation will be used?

✔ What clothing/equipment do I need to bring?

✔ What will I actually have to carry with me each day?

✔ Will there be time for sightseeing along the way?

Who are pilgrimages for?

It helps to be a follower of the relevant religion but it isn't essential.

Pros

- A pilgrimage to Santiago de Compostela is good for the body and the mind as well as the spirit.

Cons

- It isn't really a pilgrimage if you don't either walk or ride a bicycle or horse – which may be beyond many people.

Where to go

The way to Santiago de Compostela (usually from Le Puy, Roncesvalles or Leon) is undoubtedly the finest real pilgrimage in Europe. Other sites of pilgrimage include Knock, Lourdes, Lisieux, Fatima, Avila, Philippi, Patmos, Assisi, San Giovani Rotondo and, of course, Rome – but not many people walk to them.

When

The focus for many pilgrims to Santiago de Compostela is the Feast of St James on July 25th but the going will be more comfortable in spring or autumn.

Price guide

The route from Le Puy can be split up into nine chunks of six or seven nights, with each section costing around £350-£400 in basic accommodation. For a week's holiday with flights and superior accommodation think in terms of £900. The cheapest way is to make use of the *refugios* every 15 km or so along the route, for which you'll pay (or donate) less than Euros 5 a night (be warned, accommodation is in dormitories, sometimes segregated by sex).

And finally

You've really got to believe in the power of mind over matter if you're going to go firewalking. Or, as Tolly Burkan prefers to explain it, mind *in* matter (**www.firewalking.com**). Apparently it's all to do with increasing blood circulation to the feet. If you want to learn how there are courses at Quinta Mae Terra close to Olhao, Portugal (**www.firemaster.nu** Tel: 00 46 44 340 570). May the force be with you!

Other Mind, Body And Spirit Holidays: Chapter 3: Holidays With Animals; Chapter 4: Sport And Adventure Holidays; Chapter 5: Educational And Working Holidays; Chapter 8: Cultural Holidays.

Chapter 7

Extreme Sports

Unusual holidays in this chapter: freediving, scuba diving, canyoning, caving, skydiving, gliding, climbing and much more.

You know how it is when you come back from holiday. The day afterwards it already seems as if months have passed and within a year you can't remember it at all. But that's not the case with extreme holidays. Here are some experiences you'll never forget (however much you might want to).

Unusual Holiday No. 35: Freediving

Jacques Mayol, in 1976, was the first to descend deeper than 100 metres on a single breath of air, the subject of the cult film *Le Grand Bleu* (well worth watching if you fancy having a go at this).

Freediving records get broken frequently so there's no point saying what the latest one is. But to give you an idea, the ball park for holding your breath underwater without moving ('static apnea') is an incredible nine minutes (six and a half for a woman) and the greatest depth reached by someone swimming down by their own effort (with fins) is over 100 metres. Using weighted 'sledges' freedivers have gone considerably further.

One of the best places in the world to train is the 30 metre Submarine Escape Training Tank (SETT) at Portsmouth (**www.deeperblue.net**). But don't aim for more than two minutes.

Further information

For the 'Zen' side of freediving take a look at
www.sfdj.com/sand/freedive.html and **www.thejacquesmayol.com**.
For general background on freediving take a look at **www.freediver.com**,
http://freedivers.com, **www.diveglobal.com**, **www.deeperblue.net**,
www.britishfreediving.org and **www.ifyoudive.com/diving/**
freediving. The website for the International Association for the
Development of Apnea (AIDA) is **www.aida-international.org**.

Some specialist operators

The International Association of Nitrox and Technical Divers (IANTD) has
introduced three freediving courses (**www.iantd.co.uk** or Tel: 01202
840366). Freedive holidays are available on Lanzarote through
www.activeadventures.co.uk Tel: 0845 838 5953. For Florida and
California take a look at **www.performancefreediving.com**.

Some questions to ask

✓ Are you really specialists in freediving or just snorkelling?
✓ How much time in the classroom? (The answer should be quite a lot.)
✓ What safety measures are in place in the event of a blackout?
✓ Will you be operating a buddy system?
✓ Will I be insured?
✓ Do I need my own equipment?

Who are freediving holidays for?

Anyone who likes a little spirituality with their physicality.

Pros

- A fraction of the equipment needed for scuba diving.
- A 'holistic' sport.

Cons

- The search for longer dives can cause blackout (always freedive with a
  'spotter' or buddy).

Where to go

When you're trying to stay down longer you need warm sea and good visibility. The south-eastern Mediterranean in summer is excellent with water temperatures around 27°C.

When

Late August/September when the water is at its warmest.

Price guide

From £50-£250 for your own equipment. The cost for a two day course in the SETT at Portsmouth (see above) is around £300. Less sophisticated courses cost around £250 for four days. Travel and accommodation is on top.

Unusual Holiday No. 36: Scuba Diving

You'll probably never approach the achievements of a Jacques Mayol or a Tanya Streeter (one of the new freedive champions). So if you're going to stay down for a while and dive deep (maybe 30 or 40 metres) you're going to need an air supply. Our own first dives with air tanks were like seeing for the first time. It's a whole new world down there – and utterly fascinating.

The best way of getting started is to join the local branch of the British Sub-Aqua Club (**www.bsac.com** Tel: 0151 350 6200). As the title says, this is a *club* and although you *can* take a BSAC qualification on holiday most people become members of their local branch and commence training in a local swimming pool. This is the cheapest way to learn and also the best – the standard at BSAC clubs is generally superb. Once you've learned to cope with British waters you'll find your holiday in the warm, non-tidal Mediterranean much easier (but don't be complacent).

But if you want to dive *only* on holiday and aren't interested in a club and its regular activities you may find PADI (Professional Association of Diving Instructors) is the certification system that suits you better. PADI (**www.padi.com**) is designed for the holiday diver and has schools all over the world.

All sports diving works on the 'buddy' system. That's to say, you dive as a pair (even when you're diving with a group) with responsibility for each other's safety. So it helps if your partner in your terrestrial life is equally enthusiastic. Dive centres can always find a buddy for solo divers but it's much more fun with someone you know well.

If you've always loved swimming and are accustomed to jumping in from the side of a pool then it will all come very easily. Millions of people have learned all over the world. If you're apprehensive, initial nerves are best overcome by a few days swimming and snorkelling before starting the course (see Chapter 4: Sport And Adventure Holidays). The whole knack is to get gradually more and more comfortable under water.

WARNING
Diving is a potentially dangerous sport. Take proper instruction. Once qualified we strongly advise you to continue diving with a club or with a certified dive centre and not to dive alone.

Further information

For general information about diving take a look at **www.scubaduba .com**. The BSAC has an excellent magazine called *Dive* in which you'll find adverts for holidays in the UK and abroad.

For information about diving in Florida take a look at **www.florida-keys .fl.us/diving.htm** or **www.fla-keys.com/diving/** or **www.floridasmart .com** (and go to diving) or **www.southfloridadiving.com**.

For California try **www.caoutdoors.com/Diving_MP.htm**. Information about a dozen or so diving holiday specialists is grouped together on **www.divechannel.co.uk**.

Some tour operators

www.oonasdivers.com Tel: 01323 648 924

www.scuba.co.uk Tel: 0800 072 8221

www.regaldive.co.uk Tel: 0870 220 1777

www.barefoot-traveller.com Tel: 020 8741 4319

www.explorers.co.uk Tel: 0845 644 7090

Some questions to ask

✓ What certification do you offer (PADI, BSAC etc)?

✓ Do your instructors speak good English?

✓ Will my initial training be in a swimming pool?

✓ Will I be insured?

✓ Where is the nearest decompression chamber?

✓ What sort of dive boat do you have?

✓ Are you equipped with oxygen in case of emergency?

✓ Will there always be someone in charge of the boat when we're diving?

Who are diving holidays for?

Diving is far more popular with men than women but there's no physical reason for that. Children can try for the PADI Jr Open Water Diver certificate from the age of 10 (maximum depth 12 metres). If you're curious to know what goes on in the seven-tenths of the planet that's covered by water then give it a go.

Pros

● A whole new dimension to beach holidays.

● The sea is the best place for getting close to wildlife.

Cons

● Potentially dangerous.

● Lots of heavy equipment to lug about.

● Boring for non-diving members of the group.

Where to go

You can get started at your nearest BSAC branch. There are some wonderful places around the UK including the Hebrides, Anglesey, Devon, Cornwall and the Isles of Scilly. Ireland also has some great diving but in northern waters the temperature is, of course, rather cold. In the Med, the Costa Brava, Majorca, Menorca, Ibiza, the Costa del Sol, the Côte d'Azur, Corsica, Sardinia, Sicily and its islands, Cyprus, Crete and Turkey are all good. Canary Islands waters are cooler than the Med in summer but warmer than most of it in winter. The Florida Keys have the longest living coral reef in the western hemisphere.

When

Diving is a lot more pleasant when the water is warm. But equipped with a drysuit you can dive in winter, too.

Price guide

Compared with many other extreme sports, diving holidays are not expensive. In the UK prices start at around £300 for a week (accommodation, air and daily boat dives) while an all inclusive week's holiday in the Mediterranean, including 10 dives, will cost around £750. A PADI Open Water qualification costs around £200 (four days). Escorted dives cost £15-£20 per dive. The cost of your own equipment (wetsuit or drysuit, buoyancy compensator, regulator etc) is expensive – if you get hooked that could set you back £1,000 or more.

Unusual Holiday No. 37: Canyoning

Canyoning is a relatively new sport. Think of it as mountaineering backwards with lots of cold water thrown in. In other words, rather than climb up a mountain you descend and – here's the clever bit – by the bed of a stream, normally a no-no in mountaineering terms. There is an extra wrinkle. The stream has to have cut right down through the rock to create a canyon, complete with all kinds of waterfalls and natural slides, which makes limestone regions (easily dissolved) the favourite. Basically you wade, swim, jump and abseil. On a hot day in an easy canyon it can be hugely pleasurable. In the really big canyons it can be terrifying. There are lots of possibilities but if you want to make a holiday of it (rather than just go once) you need the Sierra de Guara in Aragon in the Spanish Pyrenees, which boasts more than a dozen canyons, including the famous Vero, Mascun, Balces, Barazil and Formiga. In the nearby Monte Perdido region there are half a dozen more. All enough to occupy a two week holiday.

This is something where – the easiest canyons aside – you have to have a guide. Even if you're a skilled alpinist you'll get more pleasure. The great fun is jumping down a waterfall into a pool at the bottom (ever seen that film *The Beach*?). But only a madman would

jump without knowing what's in the pool (we're not thinking croco-
diles, we're thinking sharp, leg breaking rocks). That's where the
guide comes in. He (or she) should have surveyed the route recently and know where jumping is safe and where it isn't.

Further information

Some specialist operators

Sierra de Guara
www.evazio.com Tel: 00 33 5 56 792 505
www.aventures-et-cie.com Tel: 00 33 2 54 830 800
www.stone-spirit.com Tel: 00 33 6 82 192 056
www.compania-de-guara.com Tel: 00 34 974 318 440
www.guara-canyoning.com Tel: 00 34 974 319 084

Cevennes
www.aventures-et-cie.com Tel: 00 33 2 54 830 800

Some questions to ask

✔ Have you surveyed the canyons recently (since the last heavy rainfall)?
✔ Do you supply all equipment?
✔ Are you specifically qualified for canyons?
✔ Will I be insured?
✔ What contingency plans are there in case someone gets injured?

Who are canyoning holidays for?

This is one of those holidays where you don't have to be mad but it certainly helps. But, with the right guide and the right canyon, any reasonably
fit person can play.

Pros

• If you want to be different, this is about as different as it gets.

Cons

• Canyons are dodgy places to have an accident. Rescue is difficult – and
  expensive.

Where to go

The Sierra de Guara in the Spanish Pyrenees (the top); the Pyrénées Orientales in France; the Cevennes in France.

When

There has to be the right amount of water, neither too much (dangerous) nor too little (no fun). Summer is generally the ideal time.

Price guide

Expect to pay around £375 for a week's canyoning including basic accommodation but with flights on top.

Unusual Holiday No. 38: Caving

Caves can be pretty boring places – dark, muddy, devoid of all life, compelling, it seems, only to people with some kind of psychological fixation concerning holes. But a few caves are different. A few caves are decorated with psychedelic stalactites and stalagmites and all kinds of weird and wonderful formations in the shape of straws and balls and crystals, sparkling in the light of a head torch like the safe at Fort Knox. While still others have been painted by prehistoric people with the outlines of hands and animals for a purpose that is now obscure. And the lure is this: you never know when a boring old tunnel is going to lead you into a chamber of fantastic treasures.

Some quite spectacular caves are very easy to access. So easy in fact that they've been commercialised with electric lights, guided tours and even boat and train rides, all of which you have to pay for. The formations may be pretty but that hardly constitutes an extreme sport. Now *real* caving involves abseiling, scrambling, laddering, climbing, crawling, and even snaking. General kit is old clothes with an overall on top, solid boots or wellies, a helmet and a head torch. If you're going to be underground for long you'll also need a waterproof bag for your lunch as well as your bits and pieces. For really tough going you'll need ropes.

If you're interested but wary there are caves that are a sort of halfway house. The Grotte l'Aguzou is the finest you'll ever come across, in the Gorges de l'Aude, near Axat in the eastern Pyrenees. Kitted out like a real speleologist and as part of a small group, you'll be guided through the unlit cave system, eating your lunch 600 metres underground. The formations are nothing short of miraculous (**www.grotte-aguzou.com** Tel: 00 33 4 68 20 45 38).

Further information

Caving is very much a club activity. If you're at all interested it's a good idea to join one because many caves are closed to individuals. At **www.caving.uk.com** you can see a list of clubs as well as read the magazine *Descent*. There's another online magazine at **www.cavediggers.com** and a forum at **www.speleomania.com**. For Italy see **www.gspgc.speleo.it** (Tel: 00 39 0522 456 803); for the USA see **www.caves.org**. There are links to caving (and other activities) at **www.adventuresportsholidays.com**.

Some specialist operators

www.exodus.co.uk Tel: 0870 240 5550
www.activitywales.com Tel: 01437 766 888
www.mountainandwater.co.uk Tel: 01873 831 825
www.yorkshiredalesguides.co.uk Tel: 01729 824 455
www.outdoorpursuits.co.uk Tel: 01626 836 808 or 07966 176 577
www.caverntours.com Tel: 00 1 866 762 2837

Some questions to ask

✓ How fit do I need to be?
✓ Will there be crawling involved?
✓ Will I get wet?
✓ What clothing/footwear should I bring?
✓ How many hours will we be underground?
✓ What is there to see?
✓ Is this suitable for children?
✓ Will I be insured?

Who are caving holidays for?

Certainly not the claustrophobic or anyone who objects to getting dirty.

Pros

- There are caves all over Britain and the world.
- Lucky amateurs can still make discoveries.

Cons

- Dirty, cold, uncomfortable and sometimes dangerous.

Where to go

In Britain: Wales, the Yorkshire Dales, the Peak District. As with canyoning, you need limestone to get decent caves, which there is aplenty in the Pyrenees around Arette la Pierre St-Martin/Isaba, the Ariège (try Comus) and the Pyrénées-Orientales. Also Andalucia; the Vercors and Isère in France; Tuscany and around Trieste in Italy. The world's highest ice caves are at the Cirque de Gavarnie, France.

When

Just about any time except rainy periods – caves are insulated from the temperature outside but not from the risk of flooding.

Price guide

Five nights in basic accommodation in the UK will cost around £200, excluding transport. On the Continent expect to pay around £600 for a week fully inclusive.

Unusual Holiday No. 39: Skydiving

As if jumping out of an aeroplane wasn't already exciting enough, now they've decided to spice the whole thing up with something called Accelerated Free Fall (AFF). In AFF you make a free fall jump *the first day*. In other words, no automatically opening mush-room shaped parachute. That would be too easy. No thrill at all. The real kick comes in hurtling towards the ground at well above the speed limit for a car whilst trying to remember which toggle to pull. Of course, they give you some instruction and practice first. And you'll also have contact with the ground via a headset. (*Which cord did you say? The green one? But I'm colour blind!*) Oh yes, and two instructors jump with you. Apparently, they can 'fly' to you and sort you out if things go wrong. Well, that's the theory, anyway.

If you want to find out if this could be for you, the easiest way is a *tandem jump*. Essentially you're attached to an instructor through a double harness arrangement. All you have to know is how to hold the 'position' – the one we've all seen in the movies, face down, arms half out, calves up. You exit the plane together at between 12,500 feet and 13,500 feet. You then freefall for about 60 seconds to about 5,000 feet, the instructor controlling everything while you 'ride' underneath him. You'll be dropping at up to 120 mph but at this sort of altitude you'll barely notice it. Once the instructor opens the chute you resume a vertical position, gliding down as fast or as slowly as you like (four to six minutes). Modern chutes are highly manoeuvrable so the old business of hitting the ground hard and rolling over is all finished. You come in much more sedately, like a glider (well, that's the plan). Most people's legs give way on landing – from relief – but the instructor sorts it all out.

Further information

Some specialist operators

www.ukskydiving.com Tel: 0870 787 4900
www.tandemjump.co.uk Tel: 01384 351 050
www.jumpwithus.co.uk Tel: 0800 083 0377
www.skylineparachuting.co.uk Tel: 0870 345 1000
www.activeskydiving.co.uk Tel: 01764 685 316
www.skydivecity.com Tel: 00 1 813 783 9399
www.skydiveempuriabrava.com Tel: 00 34 972 450 111
www.caladventures.com/AirAdventuresWest.htm Tel: 00 1 800 423 8908

Some questions to ask

✓ What qualifications do your instructors have?
✓ What is your accident record?

✓ What aircraft are you using?

✓ What happens if the weather conditions aren't suitable?

✓ Is the price fully inclusive of equipment and a video?

✓ Is there a weight limit?

✓ What happens if I begin falling out of control?

✓ Will I be insured?

Who are skydiving holidays for?

Adrenaline junkies with money.

Pros

● If you're hooked on adrenaline this is one of the most exciting things you can do.

Cons

● Waiting around for suitable conditions can be boring.

● Jumps don't actually last very long.

● The (very slight) possibility of dying.

Where to go

There are over 20 centres all over the UK. The acknowledged centre for skydiving in Europe is Skydive Empuriabrava on Spain's Costa Brava (contact details above). Florida. California.

When

Summer is best in Europe. In Florida avoid the hurricane season (June to November) or you might end up in New York.

Price guide

A tandem jump in the UK will cost from around £175 up to about £250. A one day Accelerated Free Fall course costs from £300 to £400. At Empuriabrava an AFF course of one tandem jump, seven AFF jumps, all instruction, loan of equipment, flights and a video of you screaming will cost around £1,000. Getting there and accommodation are on top. The good news is that once you're qualified, jumps cost around £15. At current exchange rates Florida and California are a little cheaper (but more expensive to get to).

Unusual Holiday No. 40: Gliding

Learning to fly an aeroplane isn't something you can do on holiday (unless you have very long holidays). We're talking months and something like £50,000. But you can learn to fly other things on holiday – gliders, hang gliders and paragliders.

There are two big differences between gliders and the others. The obvious one is that gliders are solid things with real seats and resemble proper aeroplanes while hang gliders and paragliders resemble the washing on a blustery day. A more important difference is that gliders, being fairly expensive things, tend to be owned and operated by clubs that aren't setting out to make a profit. The smaller clubs are run entirely by enthusiasts and only fly at weekends while others employ professional instructors, are at it most days of the year, have accommodation and are well set up for holidays. Hang gliding and paragliding, on the other hand, are run on an entirely commercial basis. Not only that, if you want to do more than just dabble on holiday you'll be expected to buy your own 'wing'. Which is kind of expensive.

But, anyway, that's not something to worry about just now. Let's get on and try the whole thing out.

Glider training is done in two seater jobs. On average you'll need about 65 launches to attain solo standard. But that doesn't mean you have to wait to get at the controls. In fact, you'll start flying on your very first launch, which is awesome.

There are two main ways of getting a glider airborne. The first is aerotow, using a powered aircraft. The other is a winch. As you can imagine, it's a lot easier to get a glider up high with aerotow. Around 2,000 feet is normal. With a winch you might get 2,000 feet but you'll more likely get a thousand and a bit (although, in fact, 3,000 feet is possible.) Aerotow is expensive. A winch is cheap.

If you've never seen a paraglider think of a parachute that not only lowers you gently down but can also lift you up (courtesy of thermals). One way of trying it out is to arrange a tandem flight. All you have to do is run a little to help the take-off. The instructor takes care of everything else. If you want a decent length flight you'll need to leap off somewhere quite high. We first tried it at Mayrhoffen, Austria, going off the edge of a staggeringly high cliff. That makes a strong impression for a start. Some people love that sense of gliding silently just above the treetops (*me, PJ*) Others like to soar up until the world below looks like Toytown then zoom down in tight spins (*me, CS*).

The usual way of getting started is on a gentle slope where you can play with your paraglider like a kite, letting it lift you a few feet off the ground. As you get more and more confident so you can go higher up the hill and try to glide for longer periods. Most schools offer introductory days where you can do this to see if the sport is for you.

The latest in ultra-light flying is the paramotor (also known as a powered paraglider). Basically it's a paraglider wing with a backpack mounted propeller driven by a two-stroke engine. They're easy to fly and if the motor should splutter to a stop you can still glide as with an ordinary paraglider. Essentially, it's a half-way house between gliding and flying.

Further information

A list of gliding clubs is available from the British Gliding Association (**www.gliding.co.uk** Tel: 0116 253 1051). For hang gliding and paragliding contact the British Hang Gliding and Paragliding Association (**www.bhpa.co.uk** Tel: 0116 261 1322).

Before going you might like to check the forecast at **www.Xcweather.co.uk** specially for ultra-light flyers.

Some specialist operators

Gliding Clubs
www.lasham.org.uk Tel: 01256 384 900
www.sussexgliding.co.uk Tel: 01825 840 764
www.logico.f9.co.uk Tel: 01869 343 265

www.gliding.utvinternet.com Tel: 07709 808 276
www.ygc.co.uk Tel: 01845 597 237
www.lakesgc.co.uk Tel: 07860 135 447

Hang gliding and paragliding
www.extremesportscafe.com for the UK and holidays in Spain
www.flyingfever.net Tel: 01770 820 292 for flying holidays on the Isle of Arran

Some questions to ask

✓ What qualifications do your instructors have?
✓ Are your instructors professionals or enthusiastic amateurs?
✓ Does your club operate every day or only at weekends?
✓ Will I be expected to assist generally?
✓ Will I have radio contact with the ground?
✓ What happens if I don't manage to get back to the airfield?
✓ Will I be insured?

Who are gliding holidays for?

The minimum age for flying a glider solo in the UK is 16 (but you can always begin training younger). Hang gliders and paragliders require an even greater feeling of immortality.

Pros

● A glider is the cheapest way of flying something that feels like a real air-craft. Hang gliders and paragliders are the cheapest way of flying something that feels like an umbrella on a windy day.

Cons

● Gliders are things you can fly now and then but the potential dangers of hang gliders and paragliders mean you need regular practice. Remember Icarus.

Where to go

The UK, France, Spain, Greece, Cyprus, Florida and California.

When

In the UK this is mostly a summer activity but it can be a winter activity, too, further south.

Price guide

Think in terms of £500 for a week's gliding course — double that for two weeks — with transport, accommodation and food on top. Some clubs do trial days at around £65. Lasham will give you a fixed price to solo of £980 with a maximum of six aerotows and all necessary winch launches up to first solo (or 12 months, whichever is sooner). If you decide to take it up as a hobby, annual memberships range from £100 up to more than £300, depending on facilities; aerotows cost around £20 per launch while a winch is about £6; time in the air is charged at about 30p a minute. For paragliding a four to five day Elementary Pilot (EP) Course will cost around £450. To go up to the next level of Club Pilot (CP) will take a further six days and cost around £350. So you could reach CP over a two week holiday. Travel, accommodation and food will be on top. If you then want to go further you'll need your own wing. That will set you back about £2,000 whilst the motorised version will be about £5,000 (halve those prices for second hand equipment).

Unusual Holiday No. 41: Climbing And Mountaineering

It's amazing to reflect how long people and mountains coexisted before anybody felt the need to climb to the top of one. The whole thing started, apparently, when a Genevese scientist called Horace-Bénédict de Saussure saw Mont Blanc in 1760 and offered prize money for the first ascent. So bizarre a challenge was it that it was nearly a quarter of a century before anyone relieved him of his money.

Nowadays everybody accepts that getting to the tops of mountains is something that, *obviously*, just has to be done. If you'd like to get to the top of Mont Blanc, western Europe's highest peak at 4,807 metres, it ain't exactly easy but it is perfectly possible. The normal way is to take the train to the Nid d'Aigle at 2,372 metres then walk/climb to the Refuge de l'Aiguille du Gouter (3,817 metres) for the night. We say 'night' but, in fact, you'll have to get up at 2 am to be on the summit before the snow melts and any summer storms set in. You'll need a guide unless you're an experienced mountain walker (**www.guides-mont-blanc.com** or **www.guides-du-montblanc.com**) and, in any case, you'll need suitable clothing, boots, crampons, ice axe and head torch and *somebody* should have a rope.

If you'd also like to bag the highest mountain in the lower 48 states of the USA then that's Mt Whitney, a slightly easier proposition than Mont Blanc and at 4,420 metres some 387 metres lower. There's no train for the first section but the trailhead, reached from Lone Pine on the east side, is at 2,550 metres. Ice axes and crampons aren't normally necessary between mid-July and October, nor are guides, but you will need a permit. See **www.nps.gov/seki/whitney.htm** for general information and then click on 'reservation information'.

Once you've climbed up something there's then the problem of getting down again. Usually there's an easy way round the back (not, unfortunately, in the case of Mont Blanc or Mt Whitney) but the smart solution is abseiling – sliding down a rope. Some people like it so much it's become an activity in its own right. The hard parts (if you don't have much of a head for heights) are hanging around for your turn and, when your turn comes, going over the edge. But after you've done it once it's really very easy. The rope passes through a friction device attached to your harness and requires very little skill on your part.

Mountaineering very definitely needs mountains but climbing doesn't. Climbing was sort of invented as a way of keeping in form in winter while waiting for better weather but is, nowadays, an activity in its own right. Of course, climbing may be an essential part of reaching a summit but it can also be done on the cliffs behind the beach, on the odd boulder or even in a gym (see Chapter 4).

A good way to test your head for all this height is a *via ferrata*.

Essentially we're talking about a climbing route on which all the hardware is permanently installed so there's no need to carry ropes and pitons and all of that. You'll be clipped onto steel cables so there's no risk if you fall and, quite often, there are fun elements like rope bridges and ladders. Grades vary but there are routes suitable for beginners as well as children. There are over 75 *via ferrata* in France (including half a dozen within easy reach of the Mediterranean coast), almost as many in Italy, 14 in Switzerland and four in Andorra (**www.viaferrata.org**).

Further information

Put 'climbing holiday' into your search engine together with the name of your chosen destination. For general information about climbing take a look at **www.abc-of-rockclimbing.com**. For information about Mont Blanc see **www.chamonix.net**. Exodus can take you around Mont Blanc and Mt Whitney but not to the summits (**www.exodus.co.uk** Tel: 0870 240 5550).

Some specialist operators

www.rockandice.net Tel: 01335 344 982
www.wild-wales.co.uk Tel: 01492 582 448
www.rockandsun.com Tel: 0871 871 6782
www.action-outdoors.co.uk Tel: 00 45 845 890 0362
www.rockandsun.com Tel: 0871 871 6782
www.colletts.co.uk Tel: 01763 289 660

Some questions to ask

✔ What experience do I require?
✔ What qualifications could I attain?
✔ If we come as a family/group will there be pitches for all levels?
✔ What equipment do I need to bring?
✔ Will I be insured?

Who are climbing holidays for?

People who understand the words 'because it is there'.

Pros

- Healthy and exhilarating with a real sense of achievement.

Cons

- Plays havoc with fingernails.
- Dangerous.

Where to go

In the UK: Scotland especially Skye, the Cairngorms, Ben Nevis and Glencoe; Wales, especially Snowdonia, the Gower and Pembrokeshire; the Lake District, Yorkshire, the Peak District, Avon Gorge, Dartmoor, Cornwall's sea cliffs, Harrison's Rocks near Tunbridge Wells. Ireland: Donegal, the cliffs at Fair Head and Sligo, the Mourne, Wicklow, Comeragh and Connemara Mountains. The Alps, especially the Mont Blanc massif and the Italian Dolomites. The Pyrenees. The Sierra Nevada in California including Mt Whitney and the Yosemite Valley.

When

Different styles of climbing can be enjoyed all year, including ice-climbing in winter.

Price guide

Think in terms of just under £100 a day on a climbing course, with travel, accommodation and food on top. A guide from the Compagnie des Guides to help you up Mont Blanc will cost around £750 for the two days for two clients. Your own basic climbing equipment (harness, helmet, rope, backpack, boots) will set you back £500 at least and with the addition of all that you'll need for mountaineering you won't see any change from £1,000.

And finally

It was Houston, Texas. We were in a plane and the plane was crashing. We could see the pilot wrestling with the controls and we could see the ground coming up to meet us. We clung to our seats and prayed. Fortunately, it was only a simulation but a simulation so realistic it was impossible to tell it from the real thing. Outside, hidden from our vision, huge hydraulic rams tilted the plane this way and that. The plane, or rather the cockpit, for that's all it was, never moved from its spot inside the hangar. And yet we were utterly convinced we were moving at hundreds of miles an hour. In California try **http://caladventures.com/ Flightline.htm**; a video briefing, a question and answer session and a half hour 'flight' will cost around £25.

Other Extreme Holidays: Chapter 12: Snow Ball Holidays.

Chapter 8

Cultural Holidays

Unusual holidays in this chapter: music festivals, arts festivals, pop festivals, literary tours, carnivals, beer festivals, tomato throwing festivals and much more.

People often say that culture is dead. Dead, that is, in the sense that national identities and traditions have all been submerged in one bland McCulture. But you only have to travel around the festivals in Europe and America to see that, if anything, cultural ideas and values are becoming even more diverse – and sometimes downright loopy.

Unusual Holiday No. 42: Music and Arts Festivals

Why go to an arts festival when – especially if you live near a large town – you could go to an 'ordinary' concert every week? The answer surely is that festivals promise an extra magic. The hope is that an unusual venue, a never-before-tried combination of performers, the freedom to experiment and the enthusiasm of the audience may make something extraordinary happen. And sometimes it does. Like Pablo Casals playing the Beethoven Sonatas at Prades in 1953. Or Sarah Vaughan at the Tivoli Gardens in Copenhagen in 1963. Or the 1970 Isle of Wight Festival with Joni Mitchell, Miles Davis, Jimi Hendrix, Joan Baez and Leonard Cohen.

To make a holiday around a festival can be quite enchanting. We'll never forget our first visit to the Peralada Festival held in the open air in the grounds of a castle in Spain (**www.festivalperalada.com**

Tel: 00 34 93 503 8646. July/August.). With tables set out in the gardens for dinner afterwards – all starched white tablecloths and candles – and with the ivy clad walls rising up behind the stage, the setting is magical. This is the kind of thing you'll never find at a concert hall.

*

There are a few 'big' ones any culture vulture will want to tick off at some time. The Edinburgh International Festival is one of them. The statistics are impressive. Over 25,000 performances of something like 1,700 shows in a total of more than 200 venues embracing classical music, opera, dance, film, theatre, exhibitions, books, talks and gigs over a three week period beginning in the middle of August. To see everything would take more than five years nonstop. The so-called Fringe, started by a few disconsolate performers not invited to the main festival, is, if anything, more famous. Anybody can perform at the Fringe, so maybe instead of just looking you should think of taking part – now that really would be an unusual holiday. For general information see **www.edinburgh festivals.co.uk**. For tickets see **www.eif.co.uk** (Tel: 0131 473 2099) and **www.edfringe.com** (Tel: 0131 226 0026).

Other festivals to be seen at least once in a lifetime include Aix-en-Provence in France in June/July (**www.festival-aix.com** Tel: 00 33 442 17 34 00); the Verona Opera Festival, mid-June to end-August, in the 1st Century AD Roman amphitheatre (**www.arena.it** Tel: 00 39 045 800 51 51); the Salzburg Summer Music Festival, late July-end August (**www.salzburgfestival.at** Tel: 00 43 662 804 55 00); and, of course, the place of pilgrimage for Wagner lovers, the Bayreuth Festival in Bavaria in July/August (**www.bayreuther-festspiele.de**).

*

It has to be said that the big festivals can nevertheless disappoint. They're so huge that, unless you've got the best tickets, you're just too far away from the action. Martin Randall Travel has got over that by organising its own private concert seasons, like the Rhine

Valley Music Festival with seven concerts in a variety of palaces, churches and theatres. The audience is limited to just 110 (**www.martinrandall.com** Tel: 020 8742 3355.)

*

Personally, we can never get comfortable at formal concerts. The seats are always so *hard*. And there's always someone annoying right in front of you. At home, listening to CDs, we lounge about on cushions, something you just can't do in the normal concert hall. So we're great fans of the Proms. For those who don't know, Prom is short for Promenade Concert, meaning that part of the Royal Albert Hall audience – the fun part – stands. There are over 1,000 standing places for each prom, and even for sell-out concerts 500 promming places are always held back for sale at the door on the day for as little as £4. The festival season of 70 or so concerts runs from mid-July until early September (**www.bbc.co.uk/proms/** Tel: 020 7589 8212).

An even better idea is to have the concert venues well spread out. Such as at opposite ends of the Orkney Islands. Then you can walk between them (**www.walkaboutscotland.com** Tel: 0131 661 7168. Late May.) And, if that still isn't enough exercise, try a Highland fling at the ceilidhs (pronounced kay-lee).

Of course, you don't have that sort of problem at a pop festival. The problem there is exactly the opposite. When do you get to stay still? Glastonbury is the largest in the world to be held in a field, or rather 900 acres of fields, in the Vale of Avalon (**www. glastonburyfestivals. co.uk** Tel: 0870 165 2005). Many years it's also the world's largest mud bath, more than a mile and a half across. There are masses of stages, featuring not just pop but also jazz, theatre, circus and cabaret.

During the three days of the festival, usually at the end of June, the standard way of getting some sleep is to bring a tent. If you want a little more luxury there's a special area designated for caravans/ camping cars. But the most luxurious accommodation on offer is Camp Kerala, run by a separate organisation and three minutes from Gate C. Fifty tents, about as luxurious as tents can be, are available. See **www.campkerala.com**.

But if you want something really anarchic you want the Isle of Wight Pop Festival, the British Woodstock (**www.isleofwight festival.org** Tel: 0870 5321 321. June.) Relive the history at **www.isleofwightfestival.com**.

Further information

For festivals in Britain see **www.artsfestivals.co.uk**. For jazz see **www.jazzservices.org.uk**. For links to major festivals all over the world see **www.somusical.com** and **www.festivals.com**. For festivals of 'world' music see **www.womad.org**. For details of music competitions all over the world contact the World Federation Of International Music Competitions (**www.wfimc.org** Tel: 00 42 23 21 36 20).

Some other music and arts festivals

Britain

www.cambridgefolkfestival.co.uk Tel: 01223 357 851 Cambridge Folk Festival. Late July.

www.hayfestival.com Tel: 0870 990 1299 Meet your favourite author in Hay, a crazy village in the Black Mountains of Wales with only 1,300 inhabitants but 39 bookshops. Ten days from late May until early June.

www.breconjazz.co.uk Tel: 01874 611 622 Brecon Jazz Festival. August. Britain's top jazz festival.

www.dokeswick.com Tel: 01900 602 122 Keswick Jazz Festival. May. Over 100 jazz events.

www.cheltenhamfestivals.co.uk Tel: 01242 262 626 Classical music, jazz, folk and literature.

www.bathfestivals.org.uk Tel: 01225 462 231 Music and literature.

www.aldeburgh.co.uk Tel: 01728 687 110 Classical music, jazz and carnival.

www.chifest.org.uk. Tel: 01243 781 312 Chichester Festival. 200 events. July.

www.buxtonfestival.co.uk Tel: 01298 72289 Buxton Opera Festival. July. In the restored Edwardian Buxton Opera House.

www.gs-festival.co.uk Tel: 01422 323 252 Buxton's Gilbert & Sullivan Festival. August.

www.thetwomoorsfestival.com Tel: 01643 831 006 Two Moors Festival. Mid-October. Exmoor/Dartmoor.

www.wayswithwords.co.uk Tel: 01803 867373 Literary festivals around the UK.

France

www.suds-arles.com Tel: 00 33 4 90 96 06 27 Arles Festival Des Musiques Du Monde. Mid-July. Over 500 concerts of music from all over the world.

www.prades-festival-casals.com Tel: 00 33 4 68 96 33 07 Prades Festival. Late July to mid August. Chamber music festival begun by cellist Pablo Casals in 1950.

www.circonautes.com Tel: 00 33 1 40 680 772 International Circus Festival of Tomorrow. Paris. January.

Belgium

www.amisduclavecin.be Tel: 00 32 016 480 836 Harpsichord festival in Brabant. Spring.

Netherlands

www.grachtenfestival.nl *Tel: 00 31 20 421 4542* August Classical music on and beside Amsterdam's canals.

Spain

www.festivalsantander.com Tel: 00 34 942 210 508. Santander Festival Internacional. All August. Music, dance and theatre in the Palacio de Festivales.

www.granadafestival.org Tel: 00 34 958 221 844. Granada Festival Internacional de Musica y Danza. End June to early July. Includes some 60 performances in the Alhambra, one of the most beautiful buildings in the world.

Portugal

www.estorilfestival.net 00 351 214 685 199 July/August.

Italy

www.newoperafestivaldiroma.com Tel: 00 39 340 088 00 77 Rome New Opera Festival. In the courtyard of the Basilica of San Clemente.

Austria

www.schubertiade.at Tel: 00 43 557 672 091 Schubertiade. Mostly in Schwarzenberg, May to August. Europe's leading chamber music festival.

Germany

www.beethovenfest.de Tel: 00 49 0180 500 1812 Bonn. September/October.

Greece

www.greekfestival.gr Tel: 00 30 210 928 2900. The Athens Festival (May-October), the Epidaurus Festival of classical drama (July/August), the Patra Festival (July-September) and much more.

USA

www.musicfestivalofthehamptons.com Tel: 00 1 800 644 4418 New York. July.

www.nycstreetfairs.com Tel: 00 1 212 809 4900 Music throughout the year on the streets of New York.

www.filmlinc.com Tel: 00 1 212 875 5050 New York Film Festival. September/October.

www.coconutgroveartsfest.com Tel: 00 1 305 447 0401 February. Florida.

www.hollywoodbowl.com Tel: 00 1 213 850 2000 Classical music, jazz and pop. June to September. California.

www.montereyjazzfestival.com Tel: 00 1 408 649 1770 World's oldest continuously running jazz festival. April. California.

www.roguefestival.com Tel: 00 1 5597 091 464 Fresno. March. California.

www.harmonyfestival.com Tel: 00 1 707 861 2035 Santa Rosa. June. Outdoor music with environmentalism. California.

www.bachfestival.org Tel: 00 1 408 624 2046 Bach festival in Carmel, California. July/August.

Some specialist operators

www.travelforthearts.co.uk Tel: 020 8799 8350
www.chambermusicholidays.co.uk Tel: 01202 528 328
www.martinrandall.com Tel: 020 8742 3355
www.archersdirect.co.uk Tel: 0870 460 3894
www.hfholidays.co.uk Tel: 020 8905 9556

Some questions to ask your operator

✔ Are all concerts included in the price or are some extra?
✔ What category are the seats?
✔ Will I have a good view?
✔ What daytime activities are included?
✔ Is transport to the concert venue included?

Who are arts and music festivals for?

Anyone who likes live performance.

Pros

● When everything comes right you'll experience something truly memorable.

Cons

● When things don't go right you'll wish you'd stayed home with a good CD.
● Some festivals provide nothing to do in the daytime.

Where to go

The list is growing all the time and many of the smaller events are more enjoyable than the famous ones.

When

Most festivals are in the summer.

Price guide

Prices of £2,000-£3,000 each are not unusual for a fully inclusive week at a European festival of classical music and opera. At the other end of the scale you can camp at a pop festival and spend no more than £100 all in.

Unusual Holiday No. 43: Carnivals And Fiestas

If you've ever wanted to throw a custard pie you can get your chance at Buñol, near Valencia. In fact, it won't be custard pies you're chucking but tomatoes, but it amounts to the same thing. On the last Wednesday in August every year hundreds of thousands of kilos are slung by tens of thousands of, mostly young, tourists in shorts and bikinis and, if they're sensible, swimming goggles. If you're wondering what this has to do with culture it's, well, La Tomatina, a festival which has now been running for 60 years (**www.comunitatvalenciana.com** Tel: 00 34 963 649 506). It seems to have started as a prank and turned into one of the most successful fiestas in Spain. Which must say something about the nature of the human race.

The fiesta begins with fireworks and all night partying. Come morning, huge lorries roll in, crammed with slushy, overripe fruit and for the next hour mayhem takes over. By the end of it, everything and everybody is coloured a vivid red – walls, windows, streets, pavements and flesh. Don't even think of going 'just to look'. This is no spectator sport. If you're not willing to get tomato into every seam and crevice then stay away. If, on the other hand, you'd enjoy looking like a pizza there's a specialist tour operator **www.latomatina.com** (Tel: 00 1 919 293 0105).

In Italy they do a similar thing with oranges, but only properly protected locals can actually do the throwing while you watch (**www.carnevalediivrea.com**).

Well, you've got to have a sense of humour, haven't you?

Anybody who says Germans have no sense of humour has never been to Munich's Oktoberfest or Cologne's Karneval. The Oktoberfest (**www.oktoberfest.de**) is the largest beer festival in the world. Every Munich brewery – there are 14 – has its own huge tent at which the horse drawn brewery wagons arrive on the first morning. They must have to go back and forth quite a few times because the festival lasts 16 days (starting on the last or the penultimate Saturday in September).

Cologne's *Karneval* is much shorter, just three days but, as they say in Cologne, they're *drei tollen Tage*. Crazy days! And they are. It's as if all inhibitions are suddenly set free and everybody – *everybody* – goes out on the streets costumed as their real selves, from clowns to reincarnations of Cleopatra (**www.colognecarnival.com** or **www.koeln.de**). It all begins on a Thursday (technically, the one prior to the seventh Sunday before Easter) with processions and costume balls. Then there's a two day lull before everything boils up to the *Rosenmontagzug* climax on the Monday, a procession featuring over a hundred bands, several hundred horses, thousands of people and probably a million sweets and chocolates thrown to the crowds. But the real spirit of carnival is what happens spontaneously on the streets and in the taverns. For an organised visit try **www.moswin.com.carnival.htm** Tel: 0870 062 5040.

We used to live just off one of the streets along which the Notting Hill Carnival passed. So we always had a happy August Bank Holiday without having to go very far. Saturday is the steel band competition, Sunday the children's carnival and Monday the big procession which, every year, has a theme. It's the largest street festival in Europe, attracting up to two million revellers (**www.lnhc.org.uk** Tel: 020 7730 3010 and **www.portowebbo.co.uk** Tel: 0870 059 1111).

If you've ever wanted to go to the Rio carnival but can't afford it then go to Loulé on the Portuguese Algarve instead (**www.cm-loule.pt** Tel: 00 351 289 400 880). They have the same *escolas de samba* and the same kinds of beautiful girls with very little on. (*Now that's my kind of carnival. PJ*)

Further information

Put 'carnival' into your search engine together with the name of the destination. For links to carnivals all over the world see
www.carnaval.com/main.htm; for events in New York see
www.nycstreetfairs.com.

Some other carnivals

www.cheeserolling.co.uk Tel: 01452 425 000 Try outrunning a rolling cheese on Coopers Hill, Gloucester.

www.caerphilly.gov.uk/bigcheese Tel: 01443 815 588 cheese, fireworks, re-enactments

www.stpatricksfestival.ie Tel: 00 353 1676 3205 St Patrick's Day celebrations. Five days from March 16th. Dublin.

www.pint.nl Tel: 00 31 10 484 8397 Bokbierfestival in Amsterdam. October.

http://carnaval.no.sapo.pt Alcobaca, Portugal.

http://carnaval.ovar.net Ovar, Portugal.

www.citalia.com Tel: 0870 909 7555. Information about the 10 day Carnevale in Venice, climaxing on Shrove Tuesday with masked balls and dancing in the Piazza San Marco. Also the Regata Storica (first Sunday in September), a procession of historic boats along the Canal Grande followed by a race for the gondoliers. For flights and accommodation see
www.veniceletsgo2.com Tel: 0871 208 3150.

www.comune.siena.it The famous horse race, the Palio, in Siena's Piazza del Campo (in July and again in August). For a tailor-made visit try
http://weekendalacarte.co.uk Tel: 0870 330 0600.

www.miamidragon.com Tel: 00 1 800 5100168 Hong Kong dragon boats in Florida.

Some questions to ask

✓ Is everything open to the public or are some events by invitation only?
✓ Where's the best place to see the action?
✓ Can I participate in the festival?
✓ What is there to do the rest of the time?

Who are carnivals and fiestas for?

If you can't find at least one to suit you you're obviously some kind of recluse.

Pros

• The chance to be completely different for a time.

Cons

• Exhaustion.

Where to go

There are carnivals and festivals everywhere.

When

The big carnival season is, of course, around Mardi Gras (French for 'fat Tuesday') which normally falls in February. But there are carnivals and fiestas all through the year.

Price guide

A six night holiday in Venice during Carnevale costs from around £350 including flights and hotel with breakfast only but excluding entry to any balls. A three night visit to the Cologne Karneval will cost around £275. A three night visit to the Palio in Siena, including the best seats in the Piazza del Campo, will cost around £1,100.

Unusual Holiday No. 44: Famous Footsteps

One of our literary heroes is Ernest Hemingway, the patron saint of all journalists. We've had quite a bit of fun looking up the places he lived and drank in Paris as well as following his footsteps around Spain. We're fans. (*Especially me. PJ*) And like all fans we want to pay homage.

For others it's Elvis Presley, or Strauss or Beethoven or Mozart. If you want to go to Memphis and see Graceland or the places associated with those other musicians take a look at **www.archersdirect. co.uk** (Tel: 0870 460 3894).

It can even be fictional characters, like Harry Potter or Robert Langdon from the DaVinci Code. Hogwart's School doesn't actually exist, of course – or does it? But in the film version, at least, it was recreated at Christ Church, Oxford. And if you want to search for those clues hidden in the Mona Lisa and various other artworks you'll need to go to Paris and visit the Louvre, St Sulpice and St Eustache. For organised visits with detailed commentary try: **www.britishtours.com** Tel: 020 7734 8734.

It's a pity you normally have to be dead before anyone shows this sort of interest in you. But a company called Chamber Music Holidays And Festivals has decided to do it differently. You can visit festivals together with musicians *who are still alive*, eat gourmet meals together with them, even jam with them if you have the ability. Locations include Corfu, Florence and Vienna (**www.chambermusicholidays.co.uk** Tel: 01202 528 328).

Further information

If you have a hero, read as much as you can, especially the autobiography, and note down the places you'd like to visit. Put the main ones into your search engine together with the word 'tour' or 'holiday' and see what comes up. At **www.literarytraveler.com** you'll find a directory of literary haunts.

Some specialist operators

www.adelanta.co.uk Tel: 0115 975 6979 chauffeured tours of literary places in England, Ireland and France.

www.holts.co.uk Tel: 01293 455 356 Battlefield tours including, for example, Poets of the Great War.

http://sfliterarytours.com Tel: 00 1 415 441 0140 The San Francisco of Allen Ginsburg, John Steinbeck, Jack Kerouac et al.

Some questions to ask

✔ Can we see inside the locations or only outside?
✔ Is this tour suitable for children?
✔ Is there a lot of walking?

Who are holidays in famous footsteps for?

Fans.

Pros

- What you've read comes to life.

Cons

- Boring for those who haven't been 'bitten'.

Where to go

Wherever your hero went.

When

Fun at any time of year.

Price guide

The one day tour of Harry Potter sites costs £250 for two; the seven day Poets of the Great War tour costs £435 per person, half board, including ferry crossing and coach. Seven days on Corfu with Chamber Music Holidays And Festivals will cost around £800 per person half board.

And finally

Europe's craziest (and oldest) festival has got to be at Cocullo in the Italian Apennines. In the days before the festival the locals go off into the surrounding mountains to search for snakes. On the day itself (the first Thursday in May) the snakes are entwined around the wooden statue of Saint Domenico as it's carried through the streets. If they stay on it will be a good year. If they slither off it will be bad. In 1984 they slid away as fast as they could. That was the year of Chernobyl. It's also pretty bad luck if you happen to grab a viper – the only one of five local species that's poisonous (**http://abruzzo2000.com/incammino/2001_0/cocullo.htm**).

Other cultural holidays: Chapter 5: Educational And Working Holidays; Chapter 11: Holidays With The Locals.

Chapter 9

Family Holidays

Unusual holidays in this chapter: cruising with children, activity holidays, theme parks you've never heard of, children's clubs, home alone (while the children go) and much more.

Holidays the whole family can go on? That's easy. Holidays the whole family can *enjoy*? Now that's a whole different story. And instead of labouring each year to find something more far-flung, more exotic (and probably more expensive) we're suggesting you sit down and look at things from a new angle. Let's face it. Mum likes lying on the beach, Dad likes golf, Johnny likes watersports and Jenny likes parties. Why fight it any longer? The average holiday just isn't going to meet all these needs. So, you've got to write your own wish lists and then find a destination that makes all the dreams come true.

Advice on the most family friendly operators can be found at specialist web sites such as **www.forparentsbyparents.com**, **www.babygoes2.com** and **www.all4kidsuk.com**. And, of course, some of the best advice on the subject comes from friends and colleagues who are in the same family boat.

Unusual Holiday No. 45: Cruising

Fewer than 150,000 children *in the whole world* go cruising every year. Which, believe it or not, is a worry to the shipping companies. And, in turn, a piece of luck for you. The fact is, shipping companies are mad keen to attract younger people onto their boats and that includes children. They are, after all, the potential cruisers of the future. To get them, many cruise lines are offering attractive prices for families. And to keep them they're doing everything possible to make sure the kids are having a good time. When you think about it, a cruise ship is just perfect. Essentially it's a compact, safe, entertainment crammed holiday resort, which – to prevent the kids ever getting bored aboard – actually *moves*.

All of the cruise lines run a variety of programmes for children of different ages. They begin with things like colouring, painting, building bricks and sing-alongs for toddlers and work up to video games, movies, plasma TVs, internet cafés and parties for teenagers. *Disney Magic and Disney Wonder,* which operate out of Miami, are obvious choices. There are packages that combine Walt Disney World with cruising the Bahamas, including Disney's private island Castaway Cay. Royal Caribbean seems to be the company that puts most emphasis on education – in a fun way, of course. Infants expand their horizons with imaginative play while older kids learn about the places they'll be visiting and do scientific experiments (but there's also a teen only nightclub).

Further information

Information about a whole variety of cruise lines is available from The Cruise People **http://members.aol.com** Tel: 020 7723 2450.

Some specialist operators

http://disneycruise.disney.go.com Tel: 020 7723 2450 / 00 I 800 95I 3532

www.carnival.com Tel: 00 I 305 406 4779

www.celebritycruises.co.uk Tel: 0845 456 I520

www.royalcaribbean.co.uk Tel: 0845 I65 84I4

www.thomson-cruises.co.uk Tel: 0870 060 2277

Some questions to ask

✓ Will there be other children for my children to play with?

✓ What on-board entertainment is there for children?

✓ Are there organised activities for children?

✔ Are there early meals for children?

✔ Can we have connecting cabins?

✔ Is there a babysitting service?

✔ Are specialist staff screened to work with children and medically trained?

Who are cruising holidays for?

Families who like everything to be taken care of.

Pros

- A pretty safe environment (no traffic, no muggings etc).

Cons

- Seasickness (but it seldom lasts long).

Where to go

The Med or the Caribbean – ports of call need to be interesting to children.

When

Summer in the Med. In the Caribbean there are two high seasons, February to mid April, and summer (but the later you go the higher the hurricane risk). Of the low season months May is a good bet.

Price guide

A family of four will pay: around £2,500 for a seven night Mediterranean cruise with Thomson; around £5,000 for a nine day Royal Caribbean fly-cruise out of Miami.

Unusual Holiday No. 46: Family Activity Holidays

There comes a time in the lives of most adolescents when the only thing more difficult than getting out of bed is getting into it. But until that all night phase arrives an activity holiday can be the ideal. Especially anything to do with beaches.

Which makes watersports holidays a good bet. Sunsail has something for just about everyone. Windsurfing, dinghies, yachts, motor boats, water-skiing. And for all levels from beginner to expert. There's the Royal Yachting Association Start Sailing course for adults and the RYA Young Sailors scheme for kids. Non-sailors can enjoy the swimming pool, beaches, tennis courts and fitness centre or join the children's clubs (Snappers 2-4 years, Sea Urchins 5-7, Gybers 8-12 and Beach Team 13-16) for everything from treasure hunts to junior discos.

Activities Abroad throws even more ingredients into the package. At Empuriabrava on the Costa Brava (a world famous skydiving centre – see Chapter 7: Extreme Holidays) you can sample not only the usual watersports but also water trekking (a combination of water based climbing, sliding, jumping and swimming), orienteering, abseiling, zip wire descents and exploring caves and creeks in sea kayaks.

Away from the beach, Exodus Travel – normally associated with grown-up serious adventure stuff – has scaled down family mountain expeditions. There's hiking, rock climbing, canyoning, mountain biking, riding, caving and canoeing in mountain streams. Camping can add even more sense of adventure. In the Ardèche region of France, Acorn Adventure Holidays has tents ready pitched native American style. That's to say, grouped together in semi-circles to enhance community spirit. Activities include canoeing and rock climbing.

For a really authentic experience try a bush craft and wilderness course. At the Woodcraft School in far-flung West Sussex you'll learn how to make camp fires, find and purify water, track and identify wildlife and all those things you've seen Ray Mears do on the telly.

But an activity holiday doesn't have to mean the back of beyond. PGL's Chateau de Grand Romaine centre is just 20 miles from the centre of Paris – close enough to accommodate a day trip to the Eiffel Tower and only a 20 minute drive from Disneyland Resort Paris (if you have any energy left over). Here you can try archery, abseiling, climbing, the high trapeze, mountain biking, orienteering or the dreaded zip wire. Parents be warned: you'll be encouraged to be the first down it – or onto the disco floor.

Further information

Some specialist operators

www.sunsail.com Tel:0870 777 0313
www.adventurecompany.co.uk Tel: 01420 541 007
www.activitiesabroad.com Tel: 01670 789 991
www.pgl.co.uk Tel: 0870 0 507 507
www.woodcraftschool.co.uk Tel: 01730 816 299
www.acornadventure.com Tel: 0800 074 9791
www.exodus.co.uk Tel: 0870 240 5550

Some questions to ask

✓ What age is this holiday suitable for?
✓ Are there specialist staff screened for working with children?
✓ Is it dangerous?
✓ Where is the nearest medical centre in case of accident?
✓ Will we be insured?

Who are family activity holidays for?

If you didn't leave it too late starting a family you might have the energy for this.

Pros

● Facing challenges together can be a great way of building family unity.

Cons

● Father/son and mother/daughter competition might be inflamed.

Where to go

Mediterranean beach based holidays are favourite.

When

Summer.

Price guide

A family of four can expect to pay: around £400 for a three day woodcraft course in West Sussex; around £1,400 for seven days on a PGL Family Active holiday using own transport or £1,700 by coach; around £3,500 for seven days at Sunsail's base at Vounaki, Greece – with special courses costing around £65 to £100 extra.

Unusual Holiday No. 47: Theme Parks You've Never Heard Of

The idea of going to a theme park may not sound very unusual. But then, there are some pretty unusual theme parks.

And here's another point. Theme parks can be a useful negotiating ploy for getting your way over a longer holiday. The kids say your chosen destination is *bor-rring*. Ah yes, you say, but there's this theme park...

Let's start with a theme park you've almost certainly never heard of. Puy du Fou? Thought not. You could call it history – the most exciting bits – brought to life. There's a Roman amphitheatre – and we're talking *big* – with gladiatorial combat and chariot racing. There's jousting. Musketeers swashing their buckles. Castles being bombarded and catching fire. Spectacular *son-et-lumière* shows. More than a thousand actors. If your children don't come away stimulated by this then they're unmoveable. Puy du Fou is in the Vendée region of France, about 45 miles south-east of Nantes.

Now let's suppose you want to go to the Auvergne. Tranquillity. Nice scenery. Long lunches. *Bor-rring!* Ah yes, but have the kids heard about Vulcania? Thought not. It has the biggest interactive earthquake simulator in Europe. Or maybe you want to see the Romanesque churches of Poitou-Charentes and stroll along the towpaths? Wait for it – *bor-rring*! Ah yes, but do the kids realise the holiday will include a visit to Futuroscope? Near Poitiers, this is the French answer to Epcot. Highlights include a 3D Space Station film, IMAX cinemas, rides and games.

In Britain, what about the Secret Bunker? Well, of course you haven't heard of it because it's a secret. It's in Scotland, near St Andrews, and is the place the great and good were going to shelter from nuclear attack while the rest of us got fried. Gullivers Theme Park at Warrington has much more than the usual rides. The kids can record their own CDs, take dance lessons, have a pop star makeover and be trained to strut the catwalk.

If you've ever wanted to see one of those Wild West bank hold-ups/shoot-outs you've no need to go as far as the USA. No further in fact than a 20 minute drive into the Tabernas Desert from Almería, Spain (see also Chapter 2: Hideaway Holidays). It was here they filmed all those 'spaghetti Westerns' like *The Good, The Bad And The Ugly*. The sets are still there in the form of Mini Hollywood/Texas Hollywood (both on the same ticket).

At the other end of Europe, near Berlin, you can see much the same gun-totin' thing at Silver Lake City, Templin, while at Babelsberg, Potsdam, you can watch stunt shows and see props from popular films. Another little known German attraction is Fort Fun in Bestwig-Wasserfall where you can all have a go at dangerous things that aren't dangerous any more (such as a Cresta Run on rails and a paraglider on cables).

In Florida there's what you could call a theme-park-for-a-day. Over the third weekend in January every year the Brooksville Raid Festival in Hernando County is the largest Civil War re-enactment in America. It involves almost four thousand actors, 24 canons and lots of horses.

But, of course, it's California that's the home of theme parks. Disneyland is the most famous but far, far from the most exciting. Try Knotts Berry Farm with its Silver Bullet ride, Paramount's Great Adventure with its Top Gun ride – experience 360 degree vertical loops and zero gravity rolls – or Six Flags Magic Mountain where you drop 255 feet to disappear into total darkness at 85 mph. If you want something gentler try Bonfante Gardens, where the 40 rides all have a horticultural theme.

Finally, not a lot of people know that New York also has an amusement park, Astroland in Brooklyn, which runs mid-March to mid-October and features one of those beautiful old roller coasters that was the start of the whole thing.

Further information

Some specialist operators

www.secretbunker.co.uk Tel: 01333 310 301 UK
www.gulliversfun.co.uk Tel: 01925 230 088 UK
www.puydufou.com Tel: 00 33 2 51 64 11 11 France
www.vulcania.com Tel: 00 33 8 20 82 78 28 France
www.futuroscope.com Tel: 00 33 5 49 49 11 12 France
www.andalucia.com Tel: 00 34 950 365 236/00 34 950 165 456 for Mini Hollywood/Texas Hollywood, Spain
www.fortfun.de Tel: 00 49 2905 810 Germany
www.filmpark.de Tel: 00 49 3317 212 755 Germany
www.silverlakecity.de Tel: 00 49 3987 20840 Germany
www.medievaltimes.com Tel: 00 1 800 229 8300 Florida
www.hernandoheritagemuseum.com Tel: 00 1 352 799 0129 Florida
www.sixflags.com Tel: 00 1 805 255 411 California
www.knotts.com Tel: 00 1 714 220 5200 California
www.pgathrills.com Tel: 00 1 408 986 1776 ext 8858 California
www.bonfantegardens.com Tel: 00 1 408 8407 100 California
www.astroland.com Tel: 00 1 718 372 025 New York

Some questions to ask

✔ Are there child care facilities?
✔ Is there a babysitting service?
✔ Is there a medical centre on site?
✔ How old/tall do you have to be for the rides?

Who are holidays at theme parks for?

Families on short breaks. Parents who need a holiday highlight for the kids.

Pros

● Designed by experts to keep children happy (and adults).

Cons

- Lots of queuing at busy times.

Where to go

California is the home of the theme park – but Europe is catching up.

When

Many theme parks are closed in winter.

Price guide

The entrance to the big American theme parks costs around £30 at the gate but there are usually special deals (such as two days for the price of one). *Quite often prices are significantly cheaper if booked online.* Futuroscope is around £22 for adults and £17 for children; Puy du Fou costs around £17 a day for adults and £10 for children; Vulcania is around £14 for adults and £9 for children.

Unusual Holiday No. 48: Children's Clubs

You know how it is. *Of course*, you want to spend the holiday together with your children (whom you don't see enough of during the week). But not *every minute* of the holiday. And especially not every evening. Well, Children's Clubs are a sort of halfway house between having holidays together and having holidays apart. You all stay in the same hotel but the kids go off and do their thing while you do yours.

Bedruthan Steps Hotel in Cornwall, close to picturesque beaches and rocky coves, is an expert in ensuring the generation gaps stays just that. There's a *Chill Out Zone* for teenagers to get away from *you* (yeah, whatever), while for younger children there are clubs called *Tadpoles, Minnows, Dolphins* and, wait for it, *Sharks*. Early suppers, evening clubs and nannies complete the parental support leaving you free to enjoy the tennis and squash courts, gymnasiums, swimming pools or just doing nothing at all. The famous Gleneagles, Perthshire also welcomes children, as long as they don't take their buckets and spades into the bunkers. Activities are more country style, including a quarter-size Land Rover. There's child friendly and then there's child mad. At the Cavallino Bianco Family Spa Grand Hotel in the *lederhosen* and pasta region of South Tyrol they almost won't let you in unless you have children. The hotel has an average of 13 childminders at any one time.

*

The whitewashed red roofed villas are typically Italian. So are the flowers, the aromas and the weather. But the music is – well what is it? It's hip-hop. But sorry parents, you can't join in. Because these hip-hop classes are only for younger guests at the Club Med in Metaponto on the Ionian coast of Southern Italy – one of 20 plus Club Med resorts worldwide. You're also barred from the karate, archery and rollerblading. But, come on, there are plenty of things for you, too, such as learning to sail, windsurf, snorkel and dive. Not to mention eat and drink (drinks are almost always included – within reason). And maybe, just maybe, later on junior will show you a few of those hip-hop moves.

*

This is how it works at Hawk's Cay Resort in the Florida Keys. You learn how to snorkel or scuba-dive, take a trip to watch dolphins in their natural habitat, study the ecology of America's longest living reef, parasail, putt and, when that's all over, steam in the spa. And the kids? Oh, they're on the pirate ship (moored in one of the five swimming pools). Can't get them off actually. At ages four and five they'll be members of Little Pirates Club and at six to 12 the Island Adventures Club. Under supervision they'll be swinging over the pool like buccaneers and climbing up to the tree house. Everybody can meet up for grub (under 12s eat free when you're in the dining room).

*

At Walt Disney World, Florida, there's all kinds of help with young-sters. The Kids' Night service (Tel: 00 1 800 696 88105 or 00 1 407 828 0920) offers babysitting in your own room at any time of day. The sitters are all over 18 years old and qualified. Reservations can be made up to two months in advance. Different hotels on site also have their own services. For example, Camp Dolphin (Tel: 00 1 407 934 4000 ext 4241) and Camp Swan (Tel: 00 1 707 934 3000 ext 1006) both provide supervised activities. Kinder-Care, based in the Administration Centre, offers day care on a drop-in basis (Tel: 00 1 407 827 5437). If you're staying at the Hyatt Grand Cypress Resort, Orlando ask about Camp Gator.

Further information

Some specialist operators

www.clubmed.com Tel: 0700 258 2932

www.virginholidays.co.uk Tel: 0870 220 2788

www.thomsonbeach.co.uk Tel: 0870 165 0079 (Ask about Superfamily and Kidzone.)

www.gleneagles.com Tel: 01764 662134

www.bedruthan.com Tel: 01637 860 860

www.hyatt.com Tel: 00 1 888 591 1234

www.cavallino-bianco.com Tel: 00 39 0471 783 333

Some questions to ask

✔ What childcare facilities are there?

✔ Are childcarers fully trained and qualified?

✔ Are children grouped according to age?

✔ Are there active options for the older kids?

✔ Are there rest facilities for the toddlers and younger?

✔ Are there babysitting facilities?

✔ Are there separate eating arrangements available?

✔ Is there medical cover for emergencies?

✔ What are the minimum/maximum ages?

✔ Can I get clothes laundered easily?

✔ Do rooms have tea making facilities and fridges?

✔ Do I have to book cots or high chairs in advance – are they an extra cost?

✔ Are there family rooms or suites?

✔ Is there somewhere comfortable to stay if there are long waits between arrival/check-in or check-out /departure?

Who are holidays with children's clubs for?

If you all like time apart each day for doing your own things this is ideal.

Pros

● Parents have time to themselves; children have fun.

Cons

● None.

Where to go

Beach resorts are favourite.

When

Summer.

Price guide

A family of four can expect to pay: around £1,500 for a fully inclusive week at the Palm Beach Club Hotel in Playa d'en Bossa, Palma, Majorca with Thomson Holidays; around £2,000 for a fully inclusive week at Club Med's Metaponto resort; around £4,000 for a fortnight at Hawk's Cay Resort with Virgin Holidays. The Kids' Night Service at WDW costs from around £8 an hour for one child up to around £12 for four or more. Supervised activities at Camp Dolphin and Camp Swan in WDW cost from about £3 an hour; Kinder-Care costs around £5 an hour or £20 a day.

Unusual Holiday No. 49: Home Alone (While The Kids Go)

Have you ever thought of *not* having a family holiday together? Of the kids going one place while you go another? Or of you staying home – all alone – and the kids going away? At first it may seem not very, well, *nurturing*, but kids only holidays are on the increase. And why not? Let's face it. Children and adults don't want to do the same things. American parents have been sending their children to Summer Camps for years so why not you? Mobile phones were invented for this kind of situation.

So while you're enjoying the peace and quiet at home, or a romantic escape (see Chapter 10) where are the kids? Camp Beaumont, one of the market leaders for this kind of thing, runs five action packed residential centres throughout the UK catering for six to 16 year olds. Most of the wide range of activities are included in the package but you have to pay extra for some specialist courses such as computers and circus skills.

If your kids are more into miming in front of the mirror than white water rafting then PGL offers a Pop Star Holiday. They'll get advice on posture, body language, presentation, singing technique and basic production skills. Then it'll be time to put on the glitter, audition, rehearse favourite songs, take part in the end-of-course concert and cut a CD to bring back to you – or perhaps send to their agent. PGL also offers an unusually wide range of energy absorbing activities.

You might feel more comfortable with a smaller, family-run centre, in which case The Mill On The Brue is perfect. There are 40 activities on site and both parents and children report high levels of satisfaction.

For genuinely athletic kids (nine to 16) Exsportise runs a variety of highly serious courses. On the *Sport and Multisport* programme they can have three hours of professional coaching each morning in their chosen sport (tennis, golf, hockey, soccer, rugby, basketball, netball, swimming or horse riding) followed by a kaleidoscope of sports in the afternoon. Or they can elect to concentrate on just one or two sports. On top of that they can have extra private lessons in the evening including – if it's an Exportise centre abroad – foreign languages.

Further information

So how do you get the little bligh…er, darlings…to agree to go? Well, of course, they may already have thought of it and want to. If not, gently float the idea well in advance by saying something cunning like: 'I hope you won't want to be going on holiday on your own now that you're older. I know those camps can be just the most fantastic fun but we're hoping you'll be joining us on our stamp collecting trip.' If they're a little nervous when the time comes Camp Beaumont has plenty of advice on its website.

Some specialist operators

www.exportise.co.uk Tel: 01444 444 777
www.pgl.co.uk Tel: 0870 050 7507
www.campbeaumont.co.uk Tel: 01263 823 000
www.millonthebrue.co.uk Tel: 01749 812 307

Some questions to ask

✓ Are all your staff screened for working with children?
✓ What steps have been taken to prevent bullying?
✓ What medical arrangements are in place to deal with illnesses and accidents?
✓ Are there qualified counsellors?
✓ Will boys and girls be sleeping well apart?
✓ Can I contact my child by mobile phone?
✓ Can my child contact me?
✓ How is pocket money dealt with?
✓ Are children allowed out of the camp?

Who are separate holidays for?

Families where the adults and kids want completely different things or where there's not enough money for everybody to go on holiday. Minimum age varies from company to company but can be as low as six for the UK, rather higher for holidays abroad.

Pros

● Everybody can do what they want without the fear of spoiling someone else's enjoyment.

Cons

● The kids may feel you're 'getting rid' of them.

Where to go

Camp Beaumont centres are based in London, Norfolk, Staffordshire and the Isle of Wight. PGL has holidays in Scotland, England, France and Italy. The Mill On The Brue is based in Somerset. Exsportise centres are at Seaford College, Claysemore School (Southampton), Sevenoaks School, Verneuil (30 km from Paris) and Marbella, Spain.

When

School holidays. Some centres operate in the summer holidays only.

Price guide

Camp Beaumont holidays cost around £400 a week all inclusive but certain special activities are around £40 extra. PGL holidays cost around £400 in the UK and £500 in France.

And finally

While you're doing your thing in London let the kids (aged nine to 16) go to *Stunt Action*. For £99 for the day they'll learn tricks of the trade from the professionals including sword and street fighting and trick flying. Or there's *Circus Space* (ages eight and upwards) to learn juggling, clowning, unicycling, break-dancing and (older children only) the high wire and trapeze. Single workshops are under £10 while introductory days cost around £25. Book online through **www.londontown.com** or **www.londonview.com**

Other Family Holidays: Chapter 1: Castaway Holidays; Chapter 3: Holidays With Animals; Chapter 4: Sport And Adventure Holidays; Chapter 5: Educational And Working Holidays; Chapter 12: Snow Ball Holidays.

Chapter 10

Romantic Holidays

Unusual holidays in this chapter: dirty weekends, fireworks, Venice the second time around, weddings and divorces, romantic train journeys, romantic roads, romantic hotels and much more.

Romantic trips come in four kinds. There's the first night in a hotel together, the classic dirty weekend. It's lust. Then there's the first serious trip away when you feel sure this is going to be it, it, it. (A ring may be in the luggage.) Next comes the honeymoon type thing. And, finally, there's the start of a whole new style of travel together. It's love.

Unusual Holiday No. 50: Dirty Weekends

For a dirty weekend abroad it's hard to beat Amsterdam, the city that invented red lights. If you have the money, head for the Grand Hotel Krasnapolsky on Dam Square (**www.nh-hotels.com** Tel: 00 31 20 554 9111). Think huge rooms for chasing round in, king-sized beds for catching in and fluffy robes for ripping open. For a romantic meal you needn't go further than the hotel's spectacular *Wintertuin* or Winter Garden, a Belle Epoque restaurant with a glass roof.

The great thing about the Kras is that the red light district is just behind the hotel, on the block west of Niewmarkt metro station. Absolutely disgraceful? You'd much prefer a good museum? Well, there's one of those. Of *erotica*, that is. Still, it is a museum. From there, move along to the sex show at the Theatre Casa Rosso. You can't miss it – it's by the 'cock and balls' fountain. If you don't want to run straight back to the hotel, the nightclub of choice for a dirty weekend has to be Sinners in Heaven (Wagenstraat 3-7 – very label conscious).

But for a really, *really* dirty weekend stay in Britain and book The Pigsty, a genuine porcine folly with a neoclassical façade built by a mad Yorkshire squire and now converted by the Landmark Trust into a little love nest for two (**www.landmarktrust.co.uk**; more follies and eccentric conversions at **www.vivat.org.uk** Tel: 0845 090 0194).

Further information

For more about Amsterdam take a look at **www.holland/com/amsterdam** or phone the Tourist Office on 00 31 20551 2525.

Some questions to ask

✓ Do you have king-size beds?
✓ Are the rooms soundproofed?
✓ Are there CD players in the rooms?
✓ Are there video/DVD players?
✓ Can we dine in our room?

Who are dirty weekends for?

Everybody should have one occasionally.

Pros

● You need to ask?

Cons

● There are none, unless you're with somebody else's partner.

Where to go

www.51-buckinghamgate.com Tel: 020 7769 7766 *51, Buckingham Gate, London.* The fact that the hotel doesn't have a proper name gives a frisson to every encounter.

www.hotelpelirocco.co.uk Tel: 01273 327 055 *Hotel Pelirocco, Regency*

Square, Brighton. The original destination for Mr and Mrs Smiths from everywhere in Britain now reinvented through this kitsch example of pop sub-culture.

www.hotelcostes.com Tel: 00 33 1 42 44 50 00 *Hotel Costes, Paris.* When you want everybody to know you're enjoying a tango in Paris this is the hyper-cool place to be seen.

www.propeller-island.com Tel: 00 49 30 891 90 16 *Propeller Island City Lodge, Berlin.* Extraordinary hotel-cum-artwork by Lars Stroschen. Ask for the diamond-shaped Mirror Room.

www.poortackere.com Tel: 00 32 9 269 2210 *Hotel Monasterium, Ghent, Belgium.* For the sheer devilment of making love in a convent.

http://andalucia.com/cavehotel/cuevas.htm Tel: 00 34 958 664 986 *Cuevas Pedro Antonio de Alarcón, Guadix, Spain.* You'll never hear the other guests and they'll never hear you in this cave hotel near Granada.

www.santorini-gr.com Tel: 00 30 22860 71983 *The Sea Captain's House, Oia, Santorini, Greece.* Bring your own shackles for the antique four-poster bed, high on the pumice cliffs on the island of Santorini.

www.libraryhotel.com Tel: 00 1 212 204 5408 *The Library Hotel, Madison Avenue, New York.* Try the Erotic Literature Room.

www.madonnainn.com Tel: 00 1 805 543 3000 *Madonna Inn, San Luis Obispo, California.* Ask for the all-pink 'Love Nest' with the spiral staircase.

When

You can never tell.

Price guide

A double room for a night with breakfast costs: from around £70 in the Propeller Island City Lodge; from around £85 in the Monasterium; from around £100 in the Grand Hotel Krasnapolsky; from around £300 in the Library Hotel. The Pigsty costs around £175 for two for a four night break.

Alternative idea

For a really *clean* weekend book into the Hotel im Wasserturm in Cologne – it was once the largest water tower in Europe **www.hotel-im-wasserturm.de** Tel: 00 49 221 200 80.

Unusual Holiday No. 51: Seeing Fireworks

Fireworks provide the perfect romantic backdrop, reflecting the way you feel when you fall in love. They zoom away up into the air, explode and then...er...fall back to Earth. Oh, well!

A combination of yachts and fireworks is hard to beat where romance is concerned. Get down to the Isle of Wight for Cowes Week at the beginning of August, charter a boat and watch the best regular firework display in England (Tel: 01983 295 744).

Hogmanay (New Year) celebrations in Edinburgh last three days *at least* (**www.edinburghshogmanay.org**). They begin with a Torchlight Procession through the streets to watch the fireworks at Carlton Hill (usually on 29th December). The famous Night Afore is a riotous street party. Then comes the big night itself, attracting one hundred thousand people from all over the world. Fireworks are launched from Edinburgh Castle and six other sites around the city. To make it a really memorable night you need tickets for the Concert in the Gardens and for the Ceilidh (pronounced kaylee) in the Assembly Rooms. If you're the more cultured sort of romantic you might prefer the Edinburgh International Festival Fireworks at the beginning of September (see **www.edinburghfestivals.co.uk**).

But the greatest *series* of fireworks displays in the *world* takes place every summer on the Rhine and Mosel (**www.germany-tourism.co.uk** Tel: 00 49 179 250 6757). The season blasts off in May when a 26 km stretch of the Rhine between Linz and Bonn is set aglow by 2000 'Bengal Fires'. Meanwhile, a fleet of 60 decorated and illuminated boats motors past and fireworks are set off at Linz, Remagen, Bad Honnef and, finally, Bonn itself.

Cologne (Koln) is a city that knows how to throw a party and the last Saturday in July is second only to the famous *Karneval* (see Chapter 8: Cultural Holidays). Again there's a parade of boats followed by a 30 minute display from a Rhine barge anchored between the Deutz and Hohenzollern bridges.

In the middle of August it's the turn of Koblenz when some 80 barges take to the river and the fireworks are set off from the Stolsenfels castle and later in the night from the Ehrenbreitstein fortress at the mouth of the Mosel.

Next comes the 10 day wine festival at Winningen, always beginning on the last Friday in August and climaxing on the Sunday of the following week with *Die Mosel in Feuerzauber*, a firework display from a boat, creating an awesome cacophony in the Mosel Gorge.

Three more displays follow at Oberwesel, St Goar and St Goarshausen before Boppard finishes the season in emphatic style with *two* wine festivals and *two* displays – on the third weekend in September (Friday to Sunday) and the following weekend.

Other firework displays to swoon to

Berlin The New Year display at the Brandenburg Gate attracts a million revellers (Tel: 00 49 30 25 00 25).

Reykjavik at New Year. Christmas lights everywhere, lots of private fireworks parties (like Britain 50 years ago) and, starting just before midnight, one of Europe's biggest fireworks displays.

France but especially Paris, on Bastille Day, 14th July.

USA on 4th July, but especially New York where Macy's has been providing the big one for more than a quarter of a century. It attracts a live audience of two million with another 12 million watching on TV (Tel: 00 1 212 695 4400). Tampa, Florida has a 4th July display lasting 20 minutes and choreographed to music as well as displays on all major holidays and Friday nights throughout the summer (Tel: 00 1 813 223 1111).

UK of course, on Guy Fawkes Night, 5th November, especially Lewes, East Sussex, noted for its subversive themes; Alexandra Palace, London; Beckenham; Eastbourne; Bolsover Castle.

Further information

A private firework show is definitely in the millionaire class (see, for example, **www.pyro-vision.com** Tel: 01883 743 335 or 01775 630 114). The smart way is to let somebody else send their money up in smoke. For a calendar of the world's major events take a look at **www.fireworks-guide.com** or for Guy Fawkes night in the UK **www.fireworks.co.uk**.

Some tour operators specialising in the Rhine/Mosel
www.noble-caledonia.co.uk Tel: 020 7752 0000
www.peter-deilmann-river.cruises.co.uk Tel: 020 7436 2931
www.travelrenaissance.com Tel: 01372 744 455
www.travelscope.co.uk Tel: 0870 380 3333
www.taberhols.co.uk Tel: 01274 594 656
www.dertravel.net Tel: 0870 142 0960
Some tour operators specialising in New York
www.virginholidays.co.uk Tel: 0870 220 2788
www.dreamusa.co.uk Tel: 0800 856 0324

Some questions to ask

✓ How long does the display last?
✓ Where is the best place to watch from?
✓ Where does everybody party afterwards?

Who are fireworks holidays for?

Romantics but also families with children.

Pros

● Everybody loves fireworks. (*I don't. CS*)

Cons

● A very short entertainment.

Where to go

See above.

When

See above.

Price guide

An all inclusive package to watch fireworks on the Rhine costs from around £500.

Unusual Holiday No. 52: Venice The Second Time Around

Venice is the most romantic city in the world and you've no doubt courted her before. But never like this. The second time around you're going to see Venice not from a gondola (at £70 for a mere 50 minutes) but from your own boat. Admittedly it will be a shade less romantic – a tub powered by an outboard motor – but it won't be much more than that for *a whole day*. And there'll be just the two of you without that gondolier chap – nice as he may be – poised on the stern like an anxious father. It's not difficult and you won't need a licence (unless you've set your heart on something big).

An even better idea could be a cabin cruiser you can sleep on (see Crown Blue Line below). That way, you can save not just the price of a gondola but the price of a hotel as well.

Just think of it. You'll tie up near Harry's Bar in Calle Vallaresso just for the hell of being where the stars go, have an ice cream at Paolin on Campo Santo Stefano, be seen at Florian on the Piazza and pay homage at the Palazzi Giustinian where Wagner wrote part of Tristan and Isolde (one of the most romantic operas ever) as well as the Palazzo Mocenigo where Byron, one of the great Romantics, lived for two years.

After that, motor gently away to the places most tourists never reach – San Michele, Murano, Burano, Torcello, San Giorgio Maggiore, Giudecca, San Lazzaro degli Armeni – in all there are 118 islands. Plus the Lagoon, the Brenta Canal and the Sile River.

Of course, you may still want that gondola ride, like Hemingway, whose infatuation with a young Venetian aristocrat led to a romantic gondola scene in *Across The River And Into The Trees*. Pay up if you insist. But there is a cheaper way. Simply take the *traghetto* or gondola ferry across the *Canal Grande*. You probably won't be on your own and you normally stand rather than sit but at least it *is* a gondola ride – and for less than 50 pence.

Further information

Some specialist boat operators
www.brussaisboat.it Tel:00 39 041 715787
www.noleggiobarchevenezia.it Tel: 00 39 041 522 9535
www.crownblueline.com Tel: 0870 160 5634

Some questions to ask

✓ Will I be able to go on the Canal Grande with this boat?
✓ Will I be able to go into the smaller canals?
✓ Where can I safely tie up?
✓ What happens if there's a problem with the boat?
✓ Will I be insured?

Who are boating holidays in Venice for?

The adventurous.

Pros

● The obvious way to see an island city.

Cons

● A boat is a responsibility.

When

Avoid summer.

Price guide

Around £90 a day for a small motorboat. From around £1,200 a week for a live-aboard cabin cruiser from Crown Blue Line.

Alternative Idea

Cruise Little Venice, London on a narrowboat from Lee Valley Boat Centre. Around £600 for a week. **www.leevalleyboats.co.uk** Tel: 01992 462 085.

Unusual Holiday No. 53: Getting Married...And Divorced

In the old days, of course, it was Gretna Green (**www.gretnawedding.com** Tel: 01461 337 971). But, nowadays, there are much more interesting places to run away to. It doesn't matter how far, just as long as the marriage is recognised in the country in which it takes place. In which case it will be recognised back home, too.

The world's most unusual wedding venue has to be Jules' Undersea Lodge in Key Largo, Florida. This tiny hotel has just two bedrooms but it's normal to book the whole place to yourselves. As you'll have to dive down using scuba gear there'll be no need to hang a 'Do Not Disturb' sign on your door. And it's unlikely your honeymoon, er, vocalisations will disturb anybody else except, maybe, a few fish. A notary public (to conduct the ceremony) and the chef (to prepare your dinner and breakfast) will come and go the same way. See **www.jul.com/weddings.htm** Tel: 00 1 305 451 2353.

Most people will probably prefer to keep their feet on dry land or, at least, sand. It certainly makes good sense to get married actually on the beach. You don't have all the aggravation of travelling before you can get on with the sunbathing. Florida (**www.partypop.com** Tel: 00 1 321 559 1012) and California (**http://ca.topweddingsites.com**) are great locations but the beach belonging to the spectacular Méridien Beach Plaza in Monaco, the only private beach in the principality, is a lot nearer (**www.meridien-plaza.monte-carlo.mc** Tel: 0800 028 28 40 – also see contact details for Weddings Abroad below).

Other Unusual Locations

New York's Central Park **www.newyorkweddings.co.uk** Tel: 01924 420 137

A cruise ship **www.pocruises.com** Tel: 0845 3555 333 or **www.royalcaribbeancruiseline.co.uk** Tel: 0800 018 2917

London Zoo **www.londonzoo.co.uk** Tel: 020 7449 6562

HMS Belfast, moored in the Thames **http://hmsbelfast.iwm.org.uk** Tel: 020 7403 6246

Liverpool Football Ground **www.liverpoolfc.tv** Tel: 0151 263 77 44

Glengorm Castle, Isle of Mull **www.glengormcastle.co.uk** Tel: 01688 302 321

And When It's All Over...

Las Vegas no longer provides the quickest divorce on the planet. The new place is the Dominican Republic on the Caribbean island of Hispaniola. Michael Jackson, Diana Ross, Sylvester Stallone, Elizabeth Taylor and Lisa Marie Presley have all made use of Dominican Divorce Law No. 142 that waives residency. It's all done in a five minute hearing, provided you *both* agree. But only one of you actually has to *go* to the island. Given its attractions, the biggest problem might be deciding who that is.

Further information

If you're using an operator specialising in weddings abroad they should know all the legal requirements. It's not a bad idea, though, to check with a Register Office in Britain or with the British Embassy or Consulate in the destination. You'll need your: birth certificates; passports; affidavits or statutory declarations that you're both single; parental consent if under age (18 or 21 depending on the country); death certificate of previous spouse if widowed; decree absolute if divorced.

Even if you get married in Britain there's no need to stick with the boring old Register Office. Nowadays, local authorities have the power to license any venues they choose.

Put 'wedding' or 'honeymoon' into your search engine together with the style of wedding (eg beach) and the name of the destination.

Some specialist operators

www.weddings.co.uk Tel: 020 7706 4848
www.weddings-abroad.com Tel: 0870 4211 062
www.goeasy-travel.com Tel: 0870 054 0220

www.honeymoonheaven.co.uk Tel: 01704 543 102/544 250
www.kuoni.co.uk/weddings Tel: 01306 747 007

Some questions to ask

✓ Have you organised a wedding in this location before?
✓ What documents do I need?
✓ How much time will it take to organise?
✓ Do I have to stay in the destination for a certain amount of time?
✓ Are you positive the wedding will be recognised in the UK?

Who are unusual wedding locations for?

Crazy people. (But, then, don't you have to be crazy to get married in the first place?)

Pros

- If you're going to spend a lot of money on one day you may as well remember it.

Cons

- Your relatives will take it as confirmation you're crazy.

Where to go

See above.

When

Soon...soon... But if you're in a real hurry, like *now* (you mad fools) take a look at **www.themarryingguy.com** Tel: 00 1 818 845 0964.

Price guide

Your wedding at Jules' Undersea Lodge – with the whole place to yourselves for one night – will cost £800. Getting married on a Royal Caribbean cruise ship will cost from around £650-£850 on top of the price of the cruise.

Unusual Holiday No. 54: Romantic Train Journeys

There's something rather romantic about a train. Not a modern train, of course, where the grubby furniture is enjoyed by just a few while everybody else stands. We're talking about old style trains. Elegant trains. Luxurious trains. The kind of trains that George Mortimer Pullman had in mind when he gave instructions that every coach should be a palace on wheels. Try telling that to train operators nowadays.

Fortunately, a few of Mr Pullman's palaces have been restored just the way he wanted them – plush upholstery, rare veneers, intricate marquetry, mosaic floors, solid brass fittings, starched tablecloths and shining silverware. Of course, these British Pullman cars, dating from the 1920s and 30s, don't operate on the 08.32 to Fenchurch Street, more's the pity. But, courtesy of the Venice Simplon-Orient Express, they are in service to such alluring destinations as Paris, Prague, Budapest, Bucharest, Istanbul and, of course, Venice (see above).

Alternatively, you could catch the Northern Belle which operates out of Manchester, Liverpool and York, or the Royal Scotsman, which chugs along the glens, lochs and stirring coastline of the Highlands.

If the prices are a little, well, too exclusive you can get a taste of what it was once like to be rich by booking a celebratory meal for Christmas, New Year or St Valentine's Day on one.

Further information

General information **www.luxury-trains.co.uk** Tel: 0870 742 0987; **www.orient-express.com** Tel: 0845 077 2222. *Train Jaune* and other French *touristiques*: **www.traintouristiques-ter.com** Tel: 00 33 8 92 35 35 35.

Some questions to ask

✓ Does the compartment have private facilities?

✓ Is a double bed possible?

✓ Will there be stops with time to take a walk or sightsee?

Who are romantic train journeys for?

Anyone who likes to spend a lot of time eating and sitting around.

Pros

● Lots of time to talk and, ahem, anything else.

Cons

● There are only single beds, one above the other.

Where to go

See above.

When

Any time.

Price guide

Romantic train journeys are staggeringly expensive. The VSOE fare from Paris to Istanbul costs almost £8,000 per couple, while London to Venice is nearly £3,000. Five nights on the Grand West Highland Tour cost around £7,000 per couple. The cheapest ways of sampling the experience are to book the hop from Venice to Rome at about £700 a couple or to celebrate Christmas/New Year/St Valentines Day with lunch/dinner at £500-£600 a couple.

Alternative Idea

For a cheaper but no less romantic journey, we'd recommend the Train Jaune from the walled Roussillon village of Villefranche-de-Conflent, dating from the 10th Century. If you go all the way to the end of the line at Latour-de-Carol, 1,200 metres up in the Pyrenees, you'll be running on the highest regular track in France. Take your own lunch in a hamper, ignore the shiny new carriages and hunker down in one of the open air barques traditionelles for a magical day out. Around £45 for the two of you.

Unusual Holiday No. 55: Romantic Highway 1

Route 66 is the world's most famous road (or rather, series of roads). Running from Chicago to Los Angeles, it's had a song and a TV series. (And just because you remember it don't let anybody say you're too old for romance.)

But 2,400 miles is a bit much for the average holiday. Instead, we nominate California's Highway 1, along the edge of the Pacific, as America's most romantic road. (And it's been in quite a few films itself.) The distance is easy (just 139 miles), the scenery breathtaking, the climate perfect, the diversions varied, the accommodation ravishing and the sunsets as romantic as it's possible to get. Book your fly-drive holiday to begin in San Francisco and finish in Los Angeles so that you're heading south with an unobstructed view of the ocean (Americans drive on the right, remember).

You can drive Highway 1 in a few hours but why hurry? Take a few days over it and stay at some of the truly romantic inns along the way such as the Post Ranch Inn (see Romantic Hotels below).

Begin at Carmel, made famous by Clint Eastwood's stint as mayor, and browse the hundred or so art studios and galleries. At nearby Pacific Grove, orange and black Monarch butterflies can be seen in their thousands between November and March. As you head south take in: Point Lobos to spot humpback whales, minke whales and sea lions; Big Sur, once home to Henry Miller, author of pioneering erotica including *Tropic of Cancer* and *Tropic of Capricorn* (why not bring one or two of his books along?); Pfeiffer Beach, one of the best on the coast; the night time hot springs at the Esalen Institute (**www.esalen.org** Tel: 00 1 831 667 3047 – don't think of staying, though, because accommodation is all in very unromantic same sex rooms and dormitories); Point Piedras Blancas with its 7,000 elephant seals; the redwoods at Limekiln Creek Canyon; beachcombing for jade on Jade Cove; La Cuesta Encantada (The Enchanted Hill) where William Randolph Hearst built Hearst Castle; otter watching in the sea below; Morro Bay, from where you can take a ferry to Spooner's Cove or visit Morro Bay State Park with its hundreds of bird species.

If you want to prolong the romance take a ferry to Catalina Island (from Long Beach, San Pedro, Newport Beach, Oceanside or San Diego). The millionaire William Wrigley named Mt Ada after his wife and built a mansion there, now a very luxurious hotel (Inn On Mt Ada, **www.catalina.com/mtada** Tel: 00 1 310 510 2030). Romance is guaranteed, provided you have a bank account like Mr Wrigley's. A no less romantic option is the Zane Grey Pueblo Hotel which the famous author of numerous westerns built for himself in pueblo style. The views are almost as good as those from Mt Ada but the price is considerably less.

The European Alternative

The *Romantische Strasse* runs for 350 km in Germany from Würzburg to Füssen. Be sure to stay at Rothenburg ob der Tauber, a perfectly preserved medieval village. Try the Burghotel, a former monastery within the walls, and the Mittermeier, just outside. Other romantic hotels along the route are the Romantik Hotel Zehntkeller at Iphofen, the Eisenkrug at Dinkelsbühl and the Schlosshotel Lisl at Hohenschwangau (**www.romantic-road.info** – also see Romantic Hotels below).

Further information

A good place to find travel information about Highway 1 is **www. californiatraveldreams.com**.

Some Fly-Drive Operators to Highway 1

www.travelcitydirect.com Tel: 0870 950 5068
www.completenorthamerica.com Tel: 0115 950 4555
www.californiaholidays.com Tel: 0845 345 0003/4
www.connectionsworldwide.co.uk Tel: 01494 473 173
www.virginholidays.co.uk Tel: 0870 220 2788
www.unitedvacations.co.uk Tel: 0870 606 2222

Some questions to ask

✓ Can I fly into San Francisco and fly out of Los Angeles?
✓ Can you book hotels for me?

✓ What happens if I have a motoring accident?

Who is Highway 1 for?

Anyone who likes the excitement of ever changing scenery.

Pros

● There's always something romantic about travelling together – a metaphor for life.

Cons

● Driving is tiring.

When to go

Less traffic in spring and autumn and even the Californian winter is nice.

Price guide

Fly-drive holidays to California cost from around £1,000 for 14 days. The Inn on Mt Ada costs around £200-£400 for two, including breakfast and lunch. A room at the Post Ranch Inn, Big Sur, costs from around £300 up to over £1,000 a night.

Unusual Holiday No. 56: Romantic Hotels

What's the most romantic building in the world? Some would say the Taj Mahal. But the most romantic building in Europe surely has to be the Alhambra in Granada. Even though you're going to have to share it with quite a lot of other people you can always find a quiet corner to sit and contemplate, hold hands and let the romance seep into your veins.

It was in AD 711 that the Moors from North Africa landed in Spain to establish what was to become one of the most cultured and wealthiest places on Earth, al-Andalus. And at its heart was the Alhambra in Granada.

From outside it looks military and impregnable, but inside is a totally different world of poetry, craftsmanship and, quite frankly, sensuality.

Which room will you choose? Perhaps the Court of the Myrtles with its mirror like pond? Or the astonishing Court of the Lions? Or maybe – yes, it has to be – the intimate Hall of Two Sisters, named after two imprisoned sisters who, it is said, died from desire after secretly observing a couple making love in a nearby garden.

Where to stay

Spain's most popular *parador* is actually inside the gardens of the Alhambra (**www.parador.es** Tel: 00 34 958 22 14 40). But there are two snags for romantics (three if you include the price). You have to book four to six months ahead (so much for spontaneity) and, oddly, none of the rooms have double beds (goodbye to, er…). A better rendezvous might be a hotel in the Albaicín, the largest Moorish quarter anywhere in Spain, on the hillside overlooking the Alhambra. The most romantic hotel here is the Casa Morisca, with just 14 rooms around an inner patio, some of which (yours) have views of the palace (**www.hotelcasamorisca.com** Tel: 00 34 958 22 11 00). The Hotel Carmen de Santa Inés also has views of the Alhambra, plus the kind of architecture that could convince you you're actually *in* the palace (**www.carmendesantaines.com** Tel: 00 34 958 226 380).

*

One other European building stands comparison with the Taj Mahal. It is the fabulous castle of Neuschwanstein in Bavaria, Germany, built by 'Mad' King Ludwig II. As he wrote to his great friend Richard Wagner, the composer, "I plan to rebuild the old castle ruin…in the true style of a German knight's castle." And he did, using Wagner's set designers to do it. Ludwig was pronounced insane in 1886 and drowned himself three days later, his fantastical castle almost, but not quite, finished.

Where to stay

The Schlosshotel Lisl, Hohenschwangau. Ask for a room with a view of Neuschwanstein (**www.lisl.de** Tel: 00 49 8 36 28 870).

Further Information

Put 'romantic hotel' into your search engine, together with the name of the destination, or try **www.hideaways.com** (Tel: 00 1 877 843 44 33); **www.historichotelsofeurope.com** (Tel: 00 33 1 5320 0830); **www .chateauxhotels.com** (Tel: 020 7616 0300); **www.serendipityrentals .com** (Tel: 0292 044 3844); **www.ghotw.com** (Tel: 0800 032 4254); **www.lhw.com** (Tel: 0800 10 10 11 11).

Ten romantic hotels in Britain

www.taychregganhotel.co.uk Tel: 01866 833 211/366 Near Oban, Scotland

www.cullodenhouse.co.uk Tel: 01463 790 461 Near Inverness, Scotland

www.hunstretehouse.co.uk Tel: 01761 490 490 Near Bath

www.burghisland.com Tel: 01548 810 514 Near Bigbury, Devon

www.gidleigh.com Tel: 01647 432 367 Chagford, Devon

www.holbeck-ghyll.co.uk 01539 432 375 Windermere, Lake District

www.amberleycastle.co.uk Tel: 01798 831 992 Near Arundel, West Sussex

www.gravetyemanor.co.uk Tel: 01342 810 567 Near East Grinstead, West Sussex

www.hafodwen.co.uk Tel: 01766 780 356 Tremadoc Bay, Wales

www.lakevyrnwy.com Tel: 01691 870 692 Llandwddyn, Wales

Ten romantic hotels in the rest of Europe

www.dromoland.ie Tel: 00 35 361 368 144 Ask for Castle Keep Cottage inside Dromoland Castle, 8 miles from Shannon Airport, Ireland

www.tinakilly.ie Tel: 00 353 40 469 274, 30 miles from Dublin, Ireland

www.marlfieldhouse.com Tel: 00 353 55 21124 County Wexford, Ireland

www.enniscoe.com Tel: 00 353 96 31112 County Mayo, Ireland

www.chateau-buronniere.com Tel: 00 33 2 4118 5698 Loire, France

www.hotel-schoenburg.com Tel: 00 49 674 493 930 Oberwesel, Rhine, Germany

www.castelletto.it Tel: 00 39 055 991 0110 Montebenichi, Tuscany

www.lesterrasses.net Tel: 00 34 971 332 643 A group of typical Ibizan cottages

www.quintaalcaidaria-mor.pt Tel: 00 351 249 542 231 Portugal

www.mykonostheoxenia.com Tel: 00 30 22890 22230 Mykonos, Greece

Ten romantic hotels in America

www.coeurdesvignes.com Tel: 00 1 631 765 2656 Long Island

http://thepointresort.com Tel: 00 1 518 891 5674/800 255 3530 Saranac Lake, New York

www.sherrynetherland.com Tel: 00 1 212 355 2800 Manhattan, New York

www.elizabethpointelodge.com Tel: 00 1 904 277 4851 Near Fernandina, Florida

www.setai.com Tel: 00 1 305 520 6000 Miami, Florida

www.pelicaninn.com Tel: 00 1 415 363 6000 Near San Francisco, California

www.mtnhomeinn.com Tel: 00 1 415 381 9000 Near San Francisco, California

www.cedargablesinn.com Tel: 00 1 707 224 7969 Napa, California

www.knickerbockermansion.com Tel: 00 1 909 878 9190 Big Bear Lake, California

www.postranchinn.com Tel: 00 1 831 667 2200 Big Sur, California

Some questions to ask

✓ Are the rooms soundproofed?
✓ What is the view from the window?
✓ Is there a CD player in the room?
✓ Can we have candles in the room?
✓ Is there a dining room with intimate and secluded tables?

Who are romantic hotels for?

Every couple, hopefully.

Pros

- This is your best chance.

Cons

- When things are going badly it can all seem a bitter joke.

Where to go

See above.

When

Sunshine is conducive to romance but too much heat isn't.

Price guide

In Granada, the Hotel Casa Morisca and the Hotel Carmen de Santa Inés both cost around £80-£165 per night per room. Castle Hotel Auf Schoenburg costs around £150 per night for the honeymoon suite with four-poster bed and double bath. Suites at Dromoland Castle cost around £700 a night.

Ten Romantic Things To Do While You're Away

- *Give chocolates from Marcolini of Belgium*. Other romantic chocolates: Belgium – Godiva, Leonidas, Neuhaus, Wittamer; Britain – Prestat; France – La Maison du Chocolat; Switzerland – Teuscher; USA – Ghirardelli.

- *Rent an airship (or light aircraft)*. And have it hover above his/her home with a banner 'PJ Loves Smithy' or whatever. About £1,000 for the day **www.blimp.co.uk** Tel: 01604 766 500.

- *Send not just any flowers*. Ask for the 'exotic arrangement' of alpina (a relative of the banana), heliconia (orange and red with beak like flowers) and strelitza (bird of paradise). Or a bunch of green roses. Either one £50. **www.serenataflower.com** Tel: 0800 083 8880.

- *Have the pianist play your favourite song* In London try The American Bar at the Savoy Hotel in the Strand (Tel: 0207 836 4343). New York is the home of the piano bar: Bemelman's Bar, 35 E 76th Street Carlyle Hotel (Tel: 00 1 212 744 1600); FireBird Café, 363 W 46th St. (Tel: 00 1 212 586 0244); Grammercy Park Hotel Bar, 2 Lexington Avenue (Tel: 00 1 212 475 4320); Top of the Tower, 3 Mitchell Place (Tel: 00 1 212 355 7300). Note that pianists don't always take kindly to being interrupted – the stylish way is to write the title on a piece of paper and ask a waiter to pass it on.

- *Swim the Hellespont* (In Greek myth Leander used to swim the Hellespont at night to visit Hero, the priestess of Aphrodite, until he drowned in a storm.) SwimTrek can recreate it for you (**www.swimtrek.com** Tel: 020 8696 6220 – see Chapter 4: Sport And Adventure Holidays).

- *Ride in a balloon* It's hard to think of a more romantic way to start the day than a hot air balloon drifting gently in the dawn sky – even if the pilot has to be there as well. Balloons Over Britain is, as it were, an umbrella organisation for 16 operators all over the country (**www.balloonsoverbritain.co.uk**). Balloon trips cost from around £125 per person for which you'll probably be in the air for an hour. But if you want it to be just the two of you (plus the pilot) you'll have to pay more like £600. At Lake Tahoe, California, they have the ultimate in style. You land on the lake on a 40 foot trimaran and enjoy breakfast while you cruise back to shore (**www.caladventures.com/Balloons OverLakeTahoe.htm** Tel: 00 1 530 544 7008; just over £100 per person).

- *Be sketched together* Try the artists who work near the National Portrait Gallery, London; or have it done from a photograph **www.canvasartists.com** or **www.jeanneelizabeth.com**.

- *Get lost together* Try Hampton Court Maze or the Great Western Maize Maze at Newton Farm near Bath (**www.greatwestern-maze.net**). Simply a-mazing!

- *Cook a romantic (aphrodisiac) meal* Going to a restaurant is so often the triumph of optimism over experience. Better to cook your own meal. Start with a salad that includes mushrooms, radishes, celery, ginger, garlic and Vadalia onions, dressed with olive oil and mustard. Substitute truffles for the mushrooms if you can afford them. Finish with angelica dipped in a sauce of melting chocolate, coffee, honey and grated vanilla. What you have in-between doesn't matter; what you do afterwards does.

- *Record your own love song* Compose a love song (or plagiarise someone else's), sing it, record it and make it into a CD, complete with personalised cover (**www.intotheblue.co.uk** Tel: 01959 578 101). Or buy software to do it at home (www.acoustica.com).

And finally

If you're one of those people who books a romantic restaurant but then gets irritated by the other diners, *Solo Per Due* (Just For Two) is the place you've been looking for. In the village of Vacone about 40 miles north of Rome it's been described as the smallest restaurant in the world. Just one table. For two people. Allow about £300 for both of you **www.soloperdue.com** Tel: 00 39 0746 676 951.

Other Romantic Holidays: Chapter 1: Castaway Holidays; Chapter 2: Hideaway Holidays; Chapter :, Mind, Body And Spirit Holidays; Chapter 12: Snow Ball Holidays.

Chapter 11

Holidays with the Locals

Unusual holidays in this chapter: pen pals, house swaps, clubs and much more.

One of the most disappointing aspects of conventional holidays is that you never get to make friends with local people. You only make contact with other holidaymakers and perhaps hotel and restaurant staff, who probably aren't local anyway. You never become immersed in the culture, learn what people's lives are like or understand what they think.

Below we give some holiday ideas that can't fail to bring you into meaningful contact with local people. But even if you don't take any of them up there are several other things everybody can do. Don't just stay with your tour group or within the hotel grounds (however diverting they may be). Don't just stick with the restaurants, bars and cafés the tourists use. Seek out the places the locals go. If you see somebody playing, say, bar billiards or *boules* then challenge them to a game. Get out and about. Throw yourself into some activity that involves local people. Be expansive and outgoing, even if it doesn't come easy to you.

Unusual Holiday No. 57: Pen Pals

Remember how, as a child encouraged by a language teacher at school, you had a pen pal abroad? You exchanged a few brief, grammatically flawed letters and then gave up. Well, now could be the time to resurrect the idea. And if your language skills aren't any better than they were then, well, just stick to English speaking pen pals.

Some internet sites are specifically dedicated to pen pals whose aim, quite openly, is to travel (for example, **www.meeturplanet. com** and **www.hospitalityclub.org**). Members post profiles of themselves on the site and establish initial contact by e-mail. Obviously you'll be hoping to meet people abroad and perhaps stay with them. But don't forget that they'll equally be wanting your companionship and help and, perhaps, to stay with you. Being a member imposes no obligation but if you want to be a traveller it's only fair that you should also be willing to be a host.

Other pen pal sites don't necessarily have cheap travel as their aim but it's only natural that, if all goes well, you'll want to visit one another.

Of course, this isn't the kind of thing to try a couple of weeks before your holiday. You need to start making contact perhaps a year in advance.

Further information

Some specialist sites

www.friendsabroad.com – essentially for pen pals to practise language skills.

www.penpalworld.com – dating as well as friendship.

www.pen-pals.net/ – dating as well as friendship.

www.europa-pages.com/penpal_form.html – a serious site, not for dating.

www.unitedplanet.org – all kinds of open discussions with people who share your interests.

WARNING

Some people use pen pal internet sites for dating and sex. Others are seeking marriage as a way of escaping a harsh economic and/or political situation. Make it very clear that you're only interested in contacting people who share your interests and outlook with a view to friendship.

Unusual Holiday No. 58: House Swapping

When you think about it, there's something inherently rather daft about holidays. They require, after all, the construction of vast amounts of accommodation that lies vacant for much of the year. It's incredibly wasteful. And there is a better way. House swapping.

Not only is it more efficient and much cheaper but you get to live in an ordinary house in an ordinary residential neighbourhood instead of in a hotel or holiday apartment. You'll have neighbours. Be able to do the things the local people do. Have the sense of really *living* in a place rather than just visiting.

Of course, if you make a simultaneous exchange you won't get to meet up with the people whose home you're moving into. But you'll probably get to meet their friends (who will have been asked to keep an eye on you). And the neighbours, too.

If you're fortunate enough to have a holiday home then you could swap that instead of your principal home. And there may be other things you could swap, too. Such as cars (so neither of you has to hire). Boats. Golf clubs. The more you think about it the better sense it all makes.

Don't rush at your house swap. They'll be wanting to feel you out and you'll be wanting to feel them out. It takes time. Think in terms of months from when you register with a house swap agency.

Different people take different attitudes to their homes. If everything in your home is precious to you then maybe you shouldn't take the risk. If, on the other hand, you take the view that friendships and experiences are more important than possessions (which can usually be replaced, anyway) then home swapping could be your thing. If you have children remember they have rights as well and can be even more possessive and territorial than adults. Explain the idea to them, involve them and make sure they're comfortable about everything before you go ahead.

However relaxed you are you'll probably have some possessions you regard as highly personal and that you'll want to lock away.

Certain clothes, perhaps, private papers, photographs, home videos – whatever. If your house is large enough you may be able to put these into a room which will then be locked. In any event, you'll have to make a certain amount of storage space available for your guests.

Once you've decided to do it try to be relaxed. A few things are bound to get broken. Just accept the idea. Budget for it. And don't get too nit-picking over quid pro quo. A perfect match is impossible. Almost inevitably one party will be getting a home slightly less luxurious than their own. If it's you just accept it philosophically.

Further information

Put 'house swap' into your search engine. With most specialist agencies you can see at least a sample of the properties registered before signing up. It helps to be flexible and interested in a range of destinations rather than just one. If you decide to go ahead, get as much advice as you can from the house swap agency and, if possible, from anybody who's done a house swap.

Some specialist agencies

www.homelink.org
www.homebase-hols.com
www.homeexchange.com
www.another-home.com
www.swapeo.com
www.swaphouse.org/eng

Some questions to ask

✓ Every kind of question to try to find out what you have in common and establish a rapport.
✓ What happens if there's a problem with either house?
✓ What about gardening and normal maintenance?
✓ What will we do about post that arrives during the holiday period?
✓ Shall we look after one another's pets?
✓ Shall we 'swap' cars, too? If yes, what about motor insurance?

✔ What about insurance for damage?

✔ What shall we do about running costs – electricity, gas and so on?

✔ What about telephones?

Who are house swap holidays for?

Anybody who doesn't mind strangers living in their home.

Pros

- A cheap holiday.
- Environmentally friendly – no empty houses.
- Hopefully your co-swappers will be looking after your house, garden and pets while you're away.

Cons

- Your home might get damaged (annoying).
- Their home might get damaged (embarrassing).

Where to go

Wherever you want.

When

Whenever you want.

Price guide

You won't be paying anything for accommodation but you'll still have to pay for fares, food etc. Membership of a home swap organisation is quite cheap – from around £30 a year up to around £75.

Unusual Holiday No. 59: Clubbing With A Difference

Clubbing has become a major part of the tourism industry, especially in destinations such as Ibiza. But that's not the sort of clubbing we're talking about. We're thinking more of professional clubs, charity clubs and special interest clubs.

We as writers, for example, are members of a couple of professional associations through which we can get in touch with members in other countries. One professional body, PEN International, exists specifically to promote friendship and understanding between writers all over the world (and, by the way, to defend freedom of expression). Lots of professions have similar bodies. When we travel we sometimes meet up. Occasionally friendships form which lead to invitations to stay. Quite probably you're a member of a professional body or a trade union. See what contacts they have with the equivalent association in your destination.

Maybe you're also a member of a special interest club at home – the Rotary Club (**www.rotary.org** – 1.2 million Rotarians in 167 countries): Lions International (**www.lionsclubs.org**), whist, bridge, poetry, yoga or whatever. Almost certainly there'll be a branch or similar club where you're going. If you're not a member of a club but nevertheless have a particular interest, put that into your search engine together with the destination. A contact name may come up. If you're a woman put 'International Women's Club' into your search engine together with your destination. Ask the local tourist office or town hall for a list of clubs in the area. If they can't help, you might see something advertised in the local supermarket or on a notice board in a specialist shop. Phone the contact number and explain that you're an enthusiast from Britain and that you'd like to join in their activities during your stay. They'll be intrigued and delighted.

And finally

It isn't easy meeting the Native Americans who live on reservations. The best way is at a powwow where you can see competitions in drumming, singing and native dress and even join in a ceremonial dance. You'll find details of powwows on **www.powwows.com**.

Other Holidays With The Locals: Chapter 3: Holidays With Animals (see Farm Holidays); Chapter 5: Educational And Working Holidays.

Chapter 12

Snow Ball Holidays

Unusual holidays in this chapter: downhill skiing, snowboarding, cross-country skiing, telemarking, dog mushing, ski-jørring, ice skating, curling and much more.

Stupid objection to winter sports holidays number one: It's too cold. After all, if it wasn't cold the snow would all melt, wouldn't it? Well, wouldn't it? Okay, yes, it *can* be cold (especially in North America). But snow can hang around even when the weather is quite warm. Being white it simply reflects the sunlight rather than absorbing it. You, on the other hand, will absorb quite a lot of heat. So, provided the sun is out, you're going to feel fine. Believe us, you'll come back with a suntan.

Stupid objection to winter sports holidays number two: There's nothing else to do apart from skiing. Okay, in some of the smaller resorts that may be the case but plenty of the larger resorts offer swimming (sometimes in heated outdoor pools), skating, curling, snowshoeing, cross country skiing, sleigh rides, trips out to the surrounding area, bars, restaurants, discos, casinos and, of course, shops.

For convenience we're describing each of the main winter sports as a distinct kind of holiday. But we'd encourage you to have a go at several of them during your one or two week stay and really enjoy a *snow ball*.

Unusual Holiday No. 60: Downhill Skiing

There's something very gay about skiing – the purple suits teamed with pink scarves and yellow hats. And that's just the men!

And it really isn't difficult. Not any more, anyway. Modern technology has created something called the parabolic ski that you can learn to turn in just a few hours. All that tricky *keep zee knees togezzer* is over – except for traditionalists. Even so, we strongly recommend ski school otherwise you'll never progress to the level where you can cope with advanced runs. Apart from anything else, there's a camaraderie about ski school that helps keep you jolly when you're falling all over the place. There's nothing better for the morale than seeing people worse than you and nothing better for the aspirations than seeing people better.

But if even parabolic skis seem daunting there's still no excuse not to go. Sorry, you're not getting out of it that easily. For you they invented ski-boards – skis that have been shrunk down to a metre or even 90 cm. The good news is they're *incapable* of going fast. And turning is a doddle. You'll be doing red (intermediate) runs within a few hours. And if you were already doing red runs you'll be on black (advanced).

*

Against this trend to make things easier a select few have started to make it all very much *harder*. To go round corners they actually *kneel* on one ski. Crazy! What they're actually doing is telemarking. But, in fact, it isn't anything new. On the contrary, this *was* skiing before the modern downhill safety binding was invented. So why would anybody want to go back to it? Well, partly for fun but also because telemark skis are much lighter. As at home on the piste as touring in the mountains.

So if they're that good why isn't everybody using them? Because holding that telemark position, like a fencer lunging, is bloody hard, that's why. It requires knees like the hinges on Tower Bridge and thighs like steel cables. Its devotees become gripped by an almost religious fervour. You may too. Give it a try.

*

In many resorts you'll see children as young as three bombing down runs in a perpetual and seemingly omnipotent snowplough. But don't be fooled. These are local children who have long been exposed to snow culture. In one or two weeks you can't expect your three year old from Flatland to do the same or even attempt it. Six is probably the earliest age you can expect a child from the plains to get interested. Send your kids to ski kindergarten or junior ski school, depending on age, and let the professionals deal with it.They'll soon make friends and falling over isn't half so bad when everybody else is doing it, too. Some child-friendly operators include: **www.ernalow.co.uk** (Tel: 0870 750 6820); **www. powderbyrne.com** (Tel: 020 8246 5300); **www.scottdunn.com** (Tel: 020 8682 5050); **www.markwarner.co.uk** (Tel: 0870 770 4228).

Further information

For general information the Ski Club of Great Britain is a good place to start **www.skiclub.co.uk**; also take a look at **www.onthesnow.com** and **www.ski-holidays.com**.You can rent equipment in the ski resort or in advance through your tour operator or try **www.snowrental.net**.

Some specialist operators

www.crystalski.co.uk Tel: 0870 160 6040

www.neilson.co.uk Tel: 0870 333 3356

www.inghams.co.uk Tel: 020 8780 4433

www.thomsonski.com Tel: 0870 888 0254

www.firstchoice.co.uk/ski Tel: 0870 850 3999

www.ifyouski.com Tel: (chalets) 0870 043 5305; (hotels) 0870 043 5306; (apartments) 0870 739 9399

www.igluski.com Tel: 020 8544 6413

www.ski-direct.co.uk Tel: 0870 017 1935

www.skimcneill.com Tel: 0870 600 1359

www.alpine-tracks.co.uk Tel: 0800 028 2546

Some telemark operators
www.pyrenees.co.uk Tel: 01635 297 209
www.telemarkskico.com Tel: 01248 810 337
www.waymarkholidays.com Tel: 01753 516 477

Some chalet specialists
www.chaletfinder.co.uk Tel: 01453 766 094
www.skichalets.co.uk Tel: 01202 503 950
www.chaletworldski.co.uk Tel: 01743 231 199

Some specialist travel agencies
www.skisolutions.com Tel: 020 7471 7700
www.alpineanswers.co.uk Tel: 020 8871 4656
www.snowfinders.com Tel: 0858 466 888
www.skimcneill.com Tel: 0870 600 1359

Some questions to ask

✔ Is this resort suitable for my level (beginner/intermediate/ advanced)?
✔ Is the snow reliable?
✔ What's the altitude of the resort? Of the top lift?
✔ Does the resort offer sufficient variety for a 1 week/2 week holiday?
✔ Can I easily ski other resorts in the area?
✔ Will I be able to use my room as soon as I arrive (and keep it until I leave)?
✔ What insurance should I have?
✔ Is there cross country skiing?
✔ Are there many drag lifts? (On drag lifts you stand up and are pulled along – not nearly as comfortable as a chairlift or cable car.)
✔ Is it crowded?
✔ What non-skiing activities are there?
✔ What is the nightlife like?

Who are ski holidays for?

Any reasonably fit adult or child.

Pros

● An invigorating getaway when British weather is at its worst.
● Snow is romantic.

Cons

- The cost of travel and accommodation is only the start of it all; there are also ski hire, lifts and lessons to pay for.

Where to go

The French Alps for good lift systems (but very little charm). The Italian Alps for long lunches and lots of posing. Austria and Switzerland for the fairy tale you always dreamed of. The Pyrenees (France, Spain and Andorra) for smaller resorts, less development but good ski touring. Don't bother with Scotland unless you live there. California for sunshine and a long season.

Some ski resorts with good shopping

St Moritz and Gstaad, Switzerland; Megève and Chamonix (France); Cortina and Madonna di Campiglio (Italy); Arcalis, Arinsal, Pas de la Casa and Soldeu for non-EU duty-free bargains (Andorra).

Some ski resorts for children

Arinsal and Soldeu in Andorra, for their English speaking instructors; Avoriaz, Flaine, Morzine, La Plagne, Puy-St-Vincent, Risoul, Les Sybelles and Valmorel in France; Heavenly and Mammoth (California).

Some ski resorts with plenty of non-ski activities

Chamonix, Megève, Morzine (French Alps); Les Angles (French Pyrenees); Bormio, Cortina d'Ampezzo, Courmayeur (Italy); Heavenly (California).

Some ski resorts with dog mushing

Flaine, Puy-St-Vincent and Tignes (French Alps); Les Angles (French Pyrenees); Cortina d'Ampezzo (Italy).

Some ski resorts with cross country skiing

Alpe'd'Huez, Avoriaz, La Clusaz, Megève, Méribel, Morzine, La Plagne, Puy-St-Vincent, St-Martin-de-Belleville, La Toussuire, La Tania and Tignes (France); Cortina d'Ampezzo, Courmayeur, Livigno, Madonna di Campiglio, Monterosa and Selva (Italy); Heavenly and Mammoth (California).

Some ski resorts with sleigh rides

Avoriaz and Morzine (France).

When

In the highest resorts the season generally opens at the beginning of December and finishes at the beginning of May (slightly later at Mammoth, California). But in the lower resorts it's much shorter. Given the unreliability of snow it makes sense to watch the snow reports and make a last minute booking. If booking ahead go for the highest resorts and, unless you like crowds, avoid Christmas to New Year and most of February.

Price guide

A week's ski holiday in Europe costs from around £300 self catering with flight up to around £1,000 full board in a good hotel. You can go to California from around £600 for a week (flight + B&B). On top of that you'll have to pay £45-£100 for equipment hire; £80-£150 (£25 for cross country) for a ski pass; and £75 for two hours ski school a day. The low season will be significantly cheaper than the high season (Christmas/New Year, February and Easter if it's early). Expect to pay around £200 extra for day long childcare.

Unusual Holiday No. 61: Snowboarding

The snowboard has transformed the winter sports scene over the past decade. Think of a surfboard or a skateboard on snow. In other words, think youth, baggy trousers, rap music... Well, that's the image, although there's no reason the middle-aged who still have their original flares tucked away in a cupboard can't do it as well. In fact, many do.

The difference between skis and snowboards can be summarised like this. Snowboards are harder at first but much easier later. What puts some people off snowboards (women more than men) is the falling over. Think of someone secretly tying your shoelaces together then pushing you. Ouch! You can feel your brains rattle. The good news is that after about a week you crash much less and after a fortnight hardly at all – by then you'll be turning circles, going backwards and carving wiggly patterns in deep snow.

Boarding comes in two styles – hard boots and soft boots. Hard boots ('alpine' style) are for fast cruising and nothing more. Soft boots are more manoeuvrable. Unless you're positive that alpine style is what you want, go for soft boots.

Further information

For operators and resorts see Unusual Holiday No. 60 pages 194–198, and see 'Where to go' below.

Who are snowboard holidays for?

The young. Also older skiers who've got stuck at the intermediate level and just can't seem to progress.

Pros

- It's easier to get good on a snowboard than it is on skis.
- Snowboards are cool.

Cons

- You fall over a lot at first and it hurts.

Where to go

The same places as for skiing (above) except (a) avoid resorts with lots of tricky drag lifts and (b) check that there's a snowpark – a boarder's playground.

When

As for skiing.

Price guide

As for skiing.

Unusual Holiday No. 62: Cross-country Skiing And Snowshoeing

If you find the *pistes* too crowded or the slopes too intimidating then maybe cross country skiing is for you. Essentially we're talking jogging on snow, generally along magnificent, tranquil and *flat* trails (well, flattish). On your feet you have lightweight boots and long, narrow skis designed for easy gliding. For a workout it's one of the finest things you can do, exercising just about every part of your body.

Snowshoes provide yet another way of getting away from the crowds and they can be as easy or demanding as you like. You can use them for strolling (not on cross country trails) or you can set off up a mountain. Look for something large in plastic with a quick and secure method of attachment – there's nothing more annoying than straps constantly working loose. For steeper work a heel lift is desirable. And a crampon.

Further information

For operators and resorts see Unusual Holiday No. 60 pages 194–198, and see 'Where to go' below.

Some questions to ask

✓ How many kilometres of cross country trails/snowshoe paths are there?
✓ What grades?
✓ Is the snow reliable? (Cross country trails are usually in the valley bottom where the snow isn't reliable.)

Who is cross country skiing/snowshoeing for?

Those searching tranquillity and solitude without the rigour of steep mountains; anyone keen on fitness.

Pros

• No expensive lift passes, no crowds, no dangerous falls.

Cons

● Hard work and none of the exhilarating speed of downhill skiing.

Where to go

Most ski resorts have at least some cross country trails but if you want to make this the focus of your holiday look at the list of ski resorts with cross country trails (above).

When

Cross country trails tend to be at lower altitude than downhill pistes so aim for February in Europe, the most reliable snow month. Or book at the last minute when you know where the snow is.

Price guide

The same as for skiing except you won't need a lift pass. The equipment is cheaper to purchase/hire, too.

Unusual Holiday No. 63: Ski Touring

Skiing on the *piste* is great fun but it just doesn't compare with touring in real snow. Going *off-piste* is one of the most ravishing things you can do. There's nothing like climbing up to a ridge or summit, experiencing the awesome views and tranquillity, maybe spotting chamois, and then gliding back down through virgin snow. You'll need specialist equipment from the hire shop, lessons in *off-piste* technique and, the first time, a guide (and for anything tricky). But you don't have to be an expert skier, merely a competent and sensible one.

Some people like to use snowboards (*me, for example. PJ*). The drawback is that you have to carry the board up on a backpack while wearing snowshoes or – if the terrain permits – tow it up. But if you've mastered the snowboard rather than skis then it's the obvious thing to do.

You could make day tours out from a centre but there's something rather special about the idea of actually *going* somewhere on skis.

In some regions you'll be able to travel from one village to another (and enjoy real food and a proper bed). Hard men (and women) stay in refuges.

AVALANCHES
The big danger off-piste is the avalanche. Resorts work tirelessly to keep their runs safe (by blowing up unstable cornices, for example) but there's nobody to do that in the wilderness. The number one rule is never to ski off-piste when the snow reports say the danger is high. You'd not just endanger your own life but also the lives of everybody below you.

Further information

For general information about ski touring take a look at **www.eagleskiclub.org.uk**; for links to specialist operators see **www.travel-quest.co.uk**.

Some specialist operators

www.alpine-guides.com Tel: 07940 407 533
www.mountaintracks.co.uk Tel: 020 8877 5773
www.peakretreats.co.uk Tel: 0870 770 0408
www.alpineadventures.co.uk Tel: 00 33 4 5054 7344
www.mountainbug.com Tel: 00 33 5629 21639
www.responsibletravel.com Online

Some questions to ask

✔ What qualifications do your guides have?
✔ How much ascent will we be doing each day?
✔ How hard are the descents?
✔ Are there any lifts we can use?
✔ What happens if there's an accident?
✔ Are you fully equipped for avalanches (avalanche transceivers, probes, shovels)?
✔ How much will I have to carry?
✔ Where will I be staying each night?
✔ Will I be insured?

Who are ski touring holidays for?

There's no escaping it, you have to be pretty fit and pretty good.

Pros

- No crowds.
- Close to nature.

Cons

- It's very hard work.
- There's always the risk of injury – or even death.

When to go

It's best to go when there's plenty of daylight – that's to say, later in the season when days are longer. Say March/April. Never go when there's a high risk of avalanche.

Where

In the Alps, Chamonix is the Mecca for ski touring if you're really good. The Pyrenees are generally kinder – the terrain is relatively easy, serious avalanches are few and there's much less development than the Alps.

Price guide

For four days off-piste expect to pay £350-£700 depending on season, including the guide and half board accommodation but not including flights, lifts or equipment hire. For six days coaching expect to pay £745.

Unusual Holiday No. 64: Dog Mushing

Dog mushing is one of the most exhilarating things you can do. Not because it's dangerous or fast but because the enthusiasm of the dogs is so infectious. We'll never forget our first time. The huskies were 'staked out' by their kennels at the top of a small rise and the sleds were at the bottom. One by one the dogs were released to run down through the snow and be attached to the ganglines of the sleds. And each time it happened the dog would be overcome with bliss, prancing, leaping, gambolling and howling joyfully at the prospect of the trip ahead. That wasn't in Scandinavia or Greenland but the sunny Pyrenees.

Note that some mushing outfits only offer short trips. To avoid disappointment check that you can do the thing properly, driving your own team behind the guide and, if you wish, staying out overnight. It isn't difficult – at least, not when there's the leader to follow.

Two alternative ways of enjoying the company of a husky (or another breed) are the pulka and ski-jørring. With a pulka (small sledge) one dog is attached in front and you're attached behind on a pair of cross country skis. In ski-jørring you dispense with the pulka and are attached to the dog via a waist belt. Watch out! Plenty of people end up face down in the snow when the dog bounds forward.

Further information

Some specialist operators
www.snowsport.highland.com/sleddogs.htm Tel: 01383 611 331
Scotland

www.saint-lary-guide.com/as_trainchien.htm France

http://fbdumoulin.free.fr/ Tel: 00 33 4 76 95 36 64 France

Husky Forever. Tel: 00 33 6 87 76 02 66 France

www.kiska-vercors.com Tel: 00 33 4 75 48 27 16 France

www.exodus.co.uk Tel: 0870 240 5550 France

www.waldschrat-adventure.de Tel: 00 49 99261731 Germany

www.husky-saas-fee.ch Tel: 00 41 7958 95804 Switzerland

Who is dog mushing for?
If you love dogs and love snow then this is for you.

Pros
● All the exhilaration of winter sports with almost no risk.

Cons
● If the snow conditions are unsuitable (too deep, too soft) it'll be a chore rather than a joy.

Where to go

French Alps and Pyrenees.

When

Whenever there's good snow.

Price guide

Unfortunately, running dog teams tends to be expensive. Expect to pay around £100 a day to drive your own team. For a two day *raid* staying in a refuge you'll pay around £225. Pulkas and ski-jørring are much cheaper.

More Fun Ideas For Your Snow Ball

Lots of resorts have *ice-skating* rinks, either indoors or out. If you'd like to try it beforehand there are 40 or so ice rinks in the UK, including four in London, and a couple each in Wales and Scotland. For general information take a look at **www.iceskating.org.uk** and **www.dotukdirectory.co.uk/Sport?Ice_Skating**.

A completely different and considerably easier way of using an ice rink is to go *curling*, played between two teams of four curlers (**www.englishcurling.co.uk**). The Royal Marine Hotel and Leisure Club in Brora, Sutherland has special weekend curling packages which cost £145 per person. See **www.highlandescapehotels.com/ reservations/packages.asp** (Tel: 01408 621 252).

Snowkiting is similar to kite-surfing, which began appearing on the beaches in 1996 (**www.flyozone.com, www.airevolution-snowkite. com**). Essentially the kite pulls you on skis or snowboard. Try Kitesurfers Center, Semnoz, Savoie **www.kitesurferscenter.com** (Tel: 00 33 4 50 52 46 21); Glisskite, Vercors **www.glisskite.com** (Tel: 00 33 6 61 43 54 23); C.Kite, Les Angles, Pyrénées Orientales **www.ckite. com** (Tel: 00 33 6 14 59 80 87). Expect to pay from around £75 for nine hours of instruction.

An *airboard* (**www.airboard.com**) is an inflatable sledge, particu-larly popular at the French resort of Les Orres in the Hautes-Alpes

(Tourist Office Tel: 00 33 4 92 44 01 61). You can also tow it behind a boat.

Most mountain *stables* send their horses down to the valleys for the winter but with Ranch El Colorado at Arc 2000 and Arc 1950 (Tel: 00 33 4 7907 0605) you can have a horse tow you along on skis (ski-joering in French). Horses can also pull a nice, comfy *sleigh*. Think of gliding between the pine trees, silent except for the jingling of the bells, to arrive at a little inn for a glass of wine. Very romantic, especially at night.

And finally

Surely any red blooded man will want to do the famous Cresta Run in St Moritz? For around £200 you can have Supplementary Membership entitling you to instruction and five rides from Junction, one-third of the way down the three-quarter mile run (**www.cresta-run.com**).The best – going from Top – get up to speeds of 80 mph The worst come off at Shuttle-cock and get to wear the Shuttlecock tie. And, sorry, ladies, apparently you're not allowed, red blooded or otherwise.

Useful contacts

You'll find all the websites referred to in this book on our website at **www.whiteladderpress.com** to make it easier for you to access them. Click on 'Useful contacts' next to the information about this book.

Contact us

You're welcome to contact White Ladder Press if you have any questions or comments for either us or the authors, or if you have any suggestions for future editions of this book. Please use whichever of the following routes suits you.

Phone: 01803 813343 between 9am and 5.30pm

Email: enquiries@whiteladderpress.com

Fax: 01803 813928

Address: White Ladder Press, Great Ambrook, Near Ipplepen, Devon TQ12 5UL

Website: **www.whiteladderpress.com**

What can our website do for you?

If you want more information about any of our books, you'll find it at **www.whiteladderpress.com**. In particular you'll find extracts from each of our books, and reviews of those that are already published. We also run special offers on future titles if you order online before publication. And you can request a copy of our free catalogue.

Many of our books have links pages, useful addresses and so on relevant to the subject of the book. You'll also find out a bit more about us and, if you're a writer yourself, you'll find our submission guidelines for authors. So please check us out and let us know if you have any comments, questions or suggestions.

Fancy another good read?

If you've enjoyed this book, you might like a taster of another of Paul Jenner and Christine Smith's books for us at White Ladder. So here's an introduction to their book **Au Revoir Angleterre** *Making a go of moving abroad.*

Maybe life in Britain is getting you down. The rain, the bills, the daily grind. There's got to be something better, surely? Suppose you lived abroad. Maybe Spain? Or perhaps the south of France? Or what about Greece? Portugal? Croatia? You'd certainly enjoy a better climate. And you'd be able to try a different way of life. It would be less stressful, healthier, cheaper, and better for the kids. You could even learn to water ski, or convert an old building, or own your own olive grove. Heaven!

Then again, you could find your problems travel with you. You miss your family and friends, you don't speak the language well enough and you can't make head nor tail of all the form filling you have to do in order to buy your dream home.

Paul Jenner and Christine Smith, expats who have lived in several countries overseas, have researched the most popular reasons Brits have for wanting to live abroad. In this book they will guide you through the pitfalls and highlights, the pros and cons of each one, so you know just what you're doing, and never regret saying 'Au Revoir Angleterre'.

Au Revoir Angleterre is priced at £9.99 and, as well as being on sale in bookshops, is available (with free p&p) from White Ladder Press on 01803 813343 or **www.whiteladderpress.com**.

Au Revoir Angleterre Extract

An affordable dream home

The Dream

You've sold your house in London, paid off the mortgage and trousered a cool £350,000 in cash. Now you're off to find a new life abroad, unburdened by debt. You spend a glorious fortnight touring Portugal and, one day, you find exactly what you've been looking for. A development of modern houses on a golf course with the use of a shared swimming pool and health spa. What's more, it's so reasonable you can pay outright and still have cash left over. You sign up. The developer pays careful attention to your special requirements and three months later, right on schedule, you're moving into your dream home.

The Reality

So are house prices actually any cheaper in, say, France or Portugal or Greece than they are in the UK? Well how about this for example? A detached house right on the beach, with four bedrooms and its own boathouse for just £275,000? Now compare that with a three bedroom property and (instead of a boathouse) a one bedroom guesthouse on an estate of 15 at £3 million. There's no comparison, you say. Yes, well, the boathouse job is in the UK – more specifically Scotland. And the estate house is on Majorca.

The fact is that if you're selling a house in London or the south-east you'll be able to buy an equivalent property in the rural parts of

France, Portugal, Spain, Italy or Greece for far less money. Or, equally, in the more remote parts of the UK, too. On the other hand, if you want to go where the millionaires sun themselves, the outer reaches of London might actually be cheaper. Yes, *cheaper*.

Broadly, there are two ways of buying a dream home abroad.
• You can buy a house that already exists.
• You can buy a house that has yet to be built.

Of the two methods, the latter is the one that gives the most problems.

Selling property 'off the plan' (in other words, it hasn't been built yet) isn't a trick and isn't specifically designed to catch foreigners. Local people also buy this way and it can make a lot of sense. You sign a contract at a fixed price for a home you can't move into for, say, six months. So by the time it's ready it's worth (with luck) considerably more than you're paying.

Spanish friends of ours bought an apartment off the plan and moved in just recently. They're very happy, not least because they made a nice profit – on paper. But the process certainly wasn't without its problems. The apartment was finished late (so they had to stay at a relative's in the meantime). And many of their stipulations regarding options and extras were either ignored or misinterpreted. Every week during the building there was a battle over something. And, don't forget, this was a Spanish couple. Buying off the plan and making the occasional trip from England to check progress you're almost *bound* to have problems.

Nor is the potential for disputes any less in the more exclusive developments where buyers are often tied up in all kinds of restrictive clauses. For example, any improvements you want subsequently may have to be carried out by the developers rather than a contractor of your own choosing. So whose dream house is it, anyway? Our advice is: *don't sign*.

In fact, according to one survey[1], nearly 60 percent of British

[1] Inmueble and Spanish Property Insight (**www.spanish-property-insight.com**).

people buying property in Spain believe they have been misled at some point. The same percentage feel that estate agents under-stated the full cost of buying and owning property in Spain. And nearly three quarters bemoaned the impossibility of getting inde-pendent advice. However, the good news is that only 3 percent were unhappy to have bought in Spain.

Part of the problem is that in countries like Spain, Italy and France, property transactions are handled by a notary, a public servant whose principal function is to collect tax for the govern-ment. So you won't find the notary much help on things like rights of way across the property, or the connection of drains, or other developments that might block the view.

On the other hand you can consult any notary for advice on prop-erty matters (not necessarily the one acting in the sale) and if you have any problems you should obviously do this well in advance of signing.

Everyone advises you to get your own lawyer. Well, that's the case in some countries but not in all. On one occasion, following the advice, we went to an *abogado*, a Spanish lawyer. He looked at us in astonishment. "But what do you want me to *do*?" he asked, spreading his hands in bewilderment. "Well," we said, "we don't know. We thought you did." It turned out that never in his life before had he been asked to get involved in a property transaction. The fact is that land and house purchases aren't treated with the same awe as in Britain. You don't have all that rigmarole for a car so why for a house?

Find out what the locals do and copy them. Even if you have a lawyer we'd still suggest you do your best to check everything for yourself with the help of a local friend or an expat who speaks the language and has already been through the process. We'd also advise:
• Never go on a trip organised by a developer.
• Never accept hospitality from a developer.
• Never sign up to any clauses that restrict your rights as a free-holder.

- Never do anything that would be crazy in Britain – like buy a timeshare from someone who approaches you in the street.

When it comes to an existing property you may have to tangle with the thorny old question of 'black'. That is, in order to reduce tax liabilities, a vendor may want to declare a sale price well below the actual price so that you pay the rest under the table. The standard advice is not to do it. Very sensible. The only problem is that, very often, you simply won't be able to buy your dream home otherwise. It's as simple as that.

Most people who have bought property in the Mediterranean can tell you funny stories about this. The way the notary suddenly has to dash out of the office for five minutes – which gives you the time to hand over the brown envelope. It's a way of life.

The declared price also has a bearing on costs. In Italy, for example, the registration fees for a house are 11 percent of the *declared* sales price. In other words, declare 300,000 euros and you'll pay 33,000 euros. Declare 200,000 euros and you'll pay 22,000 euros. In Greece purchase costs can be as high as 18 percent.

So how *do* you go about it all? The most important thing is *don't rush*. Maybe you risk losing a property but there will always be plenty of others. Don't talk to just one agent, talk to lots of agents. If you're interested in a new unit in a particular development speak to people who already live there. Ask them if their unit was completed on time, at the agreed price and to the agreed specification. And, of course, talk to the town hall about developments in the area. A lot of places are changing very fast. What you see today is not what you'll be seeing out of your windows next year. Don't just see the area on a sunny spring day. Make sure you understand what it's like in the heat of the summer and the cold of winter and during a storm. It's not just money we're talking about. It's your dream. So work on it.

Personally, we would never buy 'off the plan' or buy from a developer. But that's us. We like to be able to see what we're getting before we part with any money. And if we wanted a brand new home we'd buy the land and get it built ourselves. There are always hard luck stories. But the reality is that most people buy with no more problems than they would have in England – and are generally far happier.

Pros

- Property prices in Mediterranean countries tend to be cheaper than in the UK.

- Property values in some areas abroad (especially parts of Greece and Spain) could grow faster than in the UK.

- Some of the new building systems are superior to those used in the UK.

- If you contract for a property not yet built the price should be fixed (make sure it is) and you stand to make an immediate profit the day you take possession.

Cons

- To benefit from low prices you have to 'discover' new areas – away from towns, beaches, ski resorts and tourist attractions. This may suit you, but it may not. If you dream of the same kind of house as most people – by the sea or in a ski resort – it probably won't be any cheaper than in the UK.

- Property abroad may go up in value more slowly than in the UK, making it difficult to move back later.

- The euro/sterling exchange rate may change unfavourably for your circumstances.

- Negotiations may have to be conducted in a foreign language.

Key questions

- Are you willing to take the risk of buying 'off the plan'? Do you have the time and money to make frequent trips to check progress? Do you have the money available to put down on a property not yet built? If not, consider buying a property already completed.

- Does it have to be a brand new house or apartment, anyway? Will a slightly used one be acceptable? In some cases, second hand homes (like second hand cars) are cheaper than new ones.

- Do you know what other developments might be taking place around you in the future?

- Have you checked to see what liability you might have for the cost of things like the development of roads and street lighting?

- Are you fully aware of the total purchase costs? They can be as high as 18 percent in Greece, for example.